A Time to Build

MOSAICA PRESS

A Time TO Build

Fascinating
New Insights
in the Torah

RABBI BARUCH DOV BRAUN

Published by Mosaica Press, Inc.
www.mosaicapress.com
info@mosaicapress.com

In memory of

Elliot Braun

אליהו בן ברוך ורבקה

Eva Lux Braun

עלא גיטל בת יצחק שמעון ודבורה

Baruch Braun

ברוך בן אברהם

Blanka Braun

רבקה בת הרב אברהם אהרן הכהן

Isaac Lux

יצחק שמעון בן פנחס

Devora Lux

דבורה בת הרב אברהם אהרן הכהן

Sandor Freud

שלמה בן אליעזר וחיה

Amalia Freud

מליא בת יוסף יהודה ורחל

JUDY AND YITZ BRAUN
Proud parents of Rabbi Baruch Dov Braun

In honor of

Thelma Wadler

In memory of

Abraham Wadler

and

Munysz and Frida Grossman

We are extremely proud of our dear son-in-law

Rabbi Baruch Dov Braun

on his accomplishment of publishing his second sefer.
May he continue to have success in all his future endeavors.

LOUIS AND CEIL GROSSMAN

In memory of my תלמיד חבר

Yehuda Frankel

משה יהודה בן מאיר אליהו

BARUCH DOV BRAUN

Our prophets emphasized over and over again the *mitzvos* between man and his fellow. The prophet Micha says:

הִגִּיד לְךָ אָדָם מַה טּוֹב וּמָה יְקֹוָק דּוֹרֵשׁ מִמְּךָ אִם עֲשׂוֹת מִשְׁפָּט וְאַהֲבַת חֶסֶד וְהַצְנֵעַ לֶכֶת עִם אֱלֹקֶיךָ

In the beginning of his prophecy, Yeshayahu says:

גַּם כִּי תַרְבּוּ תְפִלָּה אֵינֶנִּי שֹׁמֵעַ יְדֵיכֶם דָּמִים מָלֵאוּ רַחֲצוּ הִזַּכּוּ הָסִירוּ רֹעַ מַעַלְלֵיכֶם מִנֶּגֶד עֵינָי חִדְלוּ הָרֵעַ

May we all heed the message of the prophets. Then, we will merit *achdus* and *shalom bayis* in our midst.

כֹּל אֲשֶׁר תֹּאמַר אֵלֶיךָ שָׂרָה שְׁמַע בְּקֹלָהּ

YOSSI AND TZIPPY PELEG BILLIG

In honor of our children

Eli, Netanel, Eitan, and Mia

You are a constant source of joy and pride.
May the light of Torah always permeate your homes
and be held in high regard.

And in honor of

Rabbi Baruch Dov Braun

Your accomplishments know no bounds.
Thank you for letting us be a part of this journey.
May you continue to inspire all of us to have a closer
relationship with Hashem and a stronger connection to Torah.

AYALAH AND DAVID JESSELSON

In honor of

Eliezer Braun

who constantly inspires our family with his strength
and positivity in face of adversity.

ADAM AND LINDSAY OKUN

In loving memory of

Zaydi and Bubbi Grossman

מנחם מוניש בן יהודה

פראדל בת יהודה לייב

Our courageous, clever, and committed grandparents,
who survived, against all odds, and in whose merit,
their children, grandchildren, and great-grandchildren
have been able to follow in their footsteps of *Yahadut*,
learning and teaching Torah.

With tremendous love, respect, and appreciation,
BECKY AND AVI KATZ AND FAMILY

In loving memory of

Rubin Krieger

אברהם ראובן בן יצחק הכהן

YOSEF AND DORIS HEIDA

In loving memory of

Mr. and Mrs. Nathan Silver

and

Mr. and Mrs. Samuel Monderer

In loving memory of

Dr. Joseph Silver

Dr. William Lerer

Dr. Isaac Belizon

In honor of our wonderful Morah D'asra

Rabbi Baruch Dov Braun

and

Our dear grandchildren

Charlotte, Oliver, Penelope and Mathew,

Zoey and Eli

May they continue and grow in their Torah learning
and acts of *chessed*.

EVELYN AND STANLEY WEISS

With appreciation and admiration to

Simone Raab Port

who commemorates and celebrates
special anniversaries this year.
Her courage and spirit created and sustained our family.

צוֹפִיָּה הֲלִיכוֹת בֵּיתָהּ וְלֶחֶם עַצְלוּת לֹא תֹאכֵל
קָמוּ בָנֶיהָ וַיְאַשְּׁרוּהָ בַּעְלָהּ וַיְהַלְלָהּ

We are eternally grateful to Hashem.

ABE, MEIR, ERIN, AND RENA PORT

לז"נ

Our dear parents

R' Shaya Strauss

ר' ישעיה ב"ר שמואל ע"ה

Vera (Lux) Strauss

מרת בונא בת ר' יצחק שמעון ע"ה

and
Our esteemed uncle and aunt

Elliot Braun

ר' אליהו ב"ר ברוך ע"ה

Eva (Lux) Braun

מרת עלא גיטל בת ר' יצחק שמעון ע"ה

May Hashem grant our cousin Rabbi Baruch Dov Braun
with the strength and wisdom to continue to inspire us
with his beautiful *divrei Torah*.

YITZCHOK AND GITTY STRAUSS AND FAMILY

RABBI NAFTALI JAEGER
ROSH HAYESHIVA

בס"ד כ"ב אלול תשע"ז

מכתב ברכה

הספר נ"ל עם פירוש בק מגולל זה משכבר לבית המדרש ובדברי הגר"א
למשלי (כה, כא) איך שלימוד התורה בפרט דמוסר ותשובה [לבית מדרש דגר"א] היא
העצה המועילה לכל התאוות והכעס ושבתורה יש שני דברים הלכות ואגדות
ועל ידי אגדות שמושך לבו של אדם מביאו ללמוד ההלכות

והנה ידידי הדבוק אל לבי הרה"ג ברוך דוד נ"י בראון [שהוא נין לגאון
בעל „הכהן הגדול מאחיו" כ"ק ת"ר ... גדולי תלמידי החת"ס) רבי מנחם
כ"ץ פרוסטיץ גאב"ד ... מגדולי תלמידי החתם סופר וז' בהעשמ"ר להשמת ספריו
משה הגאון עמוד ההוראה רבי שמואל וואזנר זצללה"ה [זצ"ל] ניכרו מאד שהחת"ס זצ"ל
אהבו אהבת נפש וגם מעשהם שמן החת"ס זצ"ל לא רצה להחזיר נשמת הקדושה
לשוע מתגברת עד שהגאון הר' מנחם כ"ץ זצ"ל לא הי' על יד מטתו לפני
הסתלקותו עש"ק - עיוה"כ [תלאי] אשר למד כמה שנים בבית מדרשנו שנו דעין ובעמילה
ונעלה ונתעלה לאילנא רברבא והוא עכשיו רב ומורה דרך בקהלה חשובה.
וגם מרביץ תורה לעדרים ביום ובלילה בגבורתנו ומעלתו אינו אלא משפיע
על קהלתו לגדול בתורה וירא שמים שלמה

והנה כתיב „לכו לחמו בלחמי ושתו ביין מסכתי" (משלי ט, ה) ופי' הגר"א
שלחמי הם הלכות וגדולי תורה ויין הוא אגדות עם דברי הגרבר
זכינו נותן לנו להשקות מיינו המשובח בשאלות אשר מושך לב כל אלו שיצאו
ללמוד אותם כדי להעלותם בסולם המדרגות של אדם המושלם מחיל אל חיל
ומעלים אנו וגם נשמה את לחמו. ידידנו הי' שהוא מחדש ומסדיר נפלא ומלמד
דברי הגמ' ורבותינו הראשונים וגדולי האחרונים ונוע חצין ללמוד. ומה גם מ'
ספרו הוא מאיר עינים ומושך דעתי שהנו רבים ממני! ובה זכה לעורר
משפחה לתפארת ולתהלה ונותן ביתו מנהג אחוה ומוסדת נפשה כדי
שלה הגדול ללמוד וללמד ולהכניס תחת כנפי השכינה ולהעמיד תלמידים הרבה.
ורצוני בזה גם לשאול להשתמש היקרים של ברכה מלומדי ומשיר אני אותם
כיעד בצע לגדל בני תורה אמיתיים ויראי ה' ויראו נחת מכל יוצאי חלציהם
מתוך בריאות מנוחת הנפש ושמחה

ובברכה ברכת הכהן שעזרי ימשיך בעבודת הקודש
להיות מרביץ תורה לעדרים ובעל רבים תלמידים ושמחת ה' בידו יצליח

בברכת כוה"ט וכט"ס
נפתלי הלוי יעגר

שאור ישוב
SH'OR YOSHUV
INSTITUTE
ONE CEDARLAWN AVENUE • LAWRENCE, NY 11559 • (516) 239-9002 • FAX: (516) 239-9003

YESHIVA UNIVERSITY

Wilf Campus, Glueck Center, Room 312 | New York, NY 10033 | Phone 212 5867007

Rabbi Dr. Michael Rosensweig
Department of Talmud

Mazer Yeshiva Program/RIETS

בס"ד
יום ב' לפרשת וירא, תשע"ח

I was exceedingly pleased to receive several chapters of Rabbi Baruch Dov Braun's forthcoming *sefer*, which contains *derashot* on *parshat ha-shavua*. The discourses are written in a clear style and thoughtful manner. They constitute insightful essays on classical and timeless issues in halakhic life that also particularly resonate in contemporary circumstances. These presentations are deeply rooted in the classical sources of the Gemara, midrash, and *parshanut* of the Rishonim, but are also effectively supplemented by later *mekorot*, as well. The works of the Seforno, Maharal, Or haHayim haKadosh, the Netziv, Rav Hirsch, Kedushat Levi, and Rav Soloveitchik, among others, are invoked to reinforce important *hashkafic* conclusions that are particularly relevant in our era.

Rabbi Baruch Dov Braun is a fine young *talmid hakham*, who is making important contributions in the world of *hinukh* and *rabbanut*. He learned diligently in our yeshivah, Yeshivat Rabbenu Yitzhak Elhanan, and he excelled as a *talmid* in my *shiur* and in the Kollel Elyon for numerous years. I am pleased to recommend his forthcoming *sefer* which projects timeless Torah values that are especially vital in our time. May he and his family continue to grow in *avodat Hashem* and *harbazat haTorah*, להגדיל תורה ולהאדירה.

בברכת התורה

מיכאל רוזנצווייג
ראש ישיבה וראש כולל
ישיבת רבינו יצחק אלחנן

For Nechama

Table of Contents

Acknowledgments

FIRST AND FOREMOST, I would like to express my gratitude to the Ribbono Shel Olam for everything that He has granted me.

It is a privilege to serve as the rabbi of Young Israel of Avenue J. Thank you to the president, Avrumie Gross, and to all the members of the shul for the close relationships we've developed over the years and for affording me the opportunity to teach and learn Torah with you. Your positive feedback regarding my *derashos* and *shiurim* encouraged me to publish them for a wider audience.

Thank you to all the generous sponsors who made this book possible: Dr. and Mrs. Mayer and Ruti Adler, Mr. and Mrs. Yossi and Tzippy Peleg Billig, Mr. and Mrs. Yitz and Judy Braun, Mr. and Mrs. Yanky and Shani Greenberg, Mr. and Mrs. Shmuel and Naomi Goldstein, Mr. and Mrs. Louis and Ceil Grossman, Rabbi and Mrs. Yosef and Doris Heida, Mr. and Mrs. David and Ayalah Jesselson, Mr. and Mrs. Avi and Becky Katz, Mr. and Mrs. Adam and Lindsay Okun, Dr. and Mrs. Abraham and Simone Port, Mr. and Mrs. Murray and Fran Puderbeutel, Mr. and Mrs. Shlomo and Barbara Rabinowitz, Drs. Leon and Rosalie Reich, Mr. and Mrs. Jerry and Barbara Schreck, Mr. and Mrs. Myron and Selina Siegel, Mr. and Mrs. Gerald and Helen Silver, Mr. and Mrs. Yitzchok and Gitty Strauss, and Dr. and Mrs. Stanley and Evelyn Weiss.

Once again, it has been a pleasure working with Mosaica Press. I am grateful to Rabbi Doron Kornbluth for his enthusiasm about this two-volume project and his editorial contributions to the manuscript. This book would not be the same if not for the dedicated and creative staff at Mosaica Press.

My dear parents have played an indispensible role throughout my life. Mom and Dad, your love for me and my family knows no bounds. From the bottom of my heart, thank you.

In addition to my parents, I am fortunate to have loving and supportive in-laws. They are gracious and generous, and they cannot hide their pride in me. Thank you, Ima and Abba.

Words cannot express the gratitude I have to Hashem for blessing me with my *eishes chayil*, Nechama. Instead, I will borrow from *Mishlei* to convey just how blessed I am: My heart relies on her and I lack no fortune. The spoils of Torah that are mine and yours, are hers. Nechama, this book is dedicated to you.

To my dear children, Shlomo, Aliza Malya, Ezra Meshulam, Menachem, Shira Fradel, Devora, and Ella Tova. The *sasson* and *simchah* you create make every day a *Yom Tov* in our home. May we continue to be a source of *nachas* for each other.

Introduction

THE TORAH IS the blueprint of the world. Consequently, the Torah is all-inclusive and spans the entire range of the human experience—from rituals and holidays to marital and criminal law to economics and politics. The very organization of the Oral Torah, the orally transmitted Word of G-d that "unpacks" and explains the Written Torah, reflects this ambitious agenda. Rabbi Yehudah HaNasi, known reverently as "Rebbi," edited and distilled the entire corpus of the Oral Torah into six diverse categories, known as Orders:

1. Agricultural law (*Zera'im*)
2. Festival law (*Moed*)
3. Marital law (*Nashim*)
4. Tort law (*Nezikin*)
5. Sacrificial law (*Kodashim*)
6. Purity law (*Taharos*)

Rebbi's need to organize vast amounts of knowledge in a way that aids memorization is readily understood. That he was able to sort all of the Oral Torah into six general categories of human enterprises is also unsurprising, especially in light of the Torah's broad ambition, mentioned above. What is not obvious, however, is his specific sequence. Why, for example, is *Zera'im* first and *Taharos* last? Why does *Nashim* precede *Nezikin*? And so on. Is this order arbitrary? Or did Rebbi arrange his list systematically? If the latter, what was his method based on, and, more importantly, what lasting insight did he intend to leave the student of the Torah?

We are not the first to be intrigued by the sequence of the Orders. The *Rambam*, in the introduction to his *Commentary on the Mishnayos*, suggests that Rebbi patterned his sequence on the Written Torah itself:

- Rebbi's starting point is *Zera'im*, because man cannot live and serve Hashem without sustenance.
- From there, Rebbi transitioned to *Moed*, because in the middle of *Sefer Shemos*, in the midst of *Parashas Mishpatim*, the laws of Shabbos and the Festivals immediately follow the agricultural laws regulating the *shemittah* year.
- *Nashim* is next, followed by *Nezikin*, since the Written Torah itself, at the beginning of *Parashas Mishpatim*, introduces the laws of damages on the heels of the laws governing a father's ability to sell or betroth his daughter.
- Rebbi's sequence concludes with *Kodashim* and *Taharos* because *Sefer Vayikra*, which comes after *Sefer Shemos* in the Written Torah, concerns itself first with sacrificial rites, followed by the laws of purity and contamination.

The *Rambam*'s theory—that Rebbi modeled his sequencing of the Oral Torah after the Written Torah—intrigued me. What if, I wondered, instead of starting in the middle of *Sefer Shemos*, Rebbi looked elsewhere in the Written Torah for inspiration, i.e., at the very beginning? Let us take a look at the creation narrative:

- On the third day of creation, after Hashem gathers the waters to expose the dry land, He creates vegetation, seeds, herbs, trees, and fruit.
- On the fourth day of creation, Hashem creates celestial bodies, the sun, moon, and stars, to be "for signs and for appointed seasons and for days and years."[1]
- Over the next two days, on the fifth and sixth days of creation, Hashem creates the entire animal kingdom, blessing the fish and birds to be "fruitful and multiply."[2]

---

1   *Bereishis* 1:14.
2   Ibid. 1:22.

- Continuing on the sixth day, Hashem fashions mankind in His image, creating them male and female, and blesses them: "Be fruitful and multiply."[3]

Even a cursory glance at the order of creation reveals something striking: The creation of vegetation is followed by the creation of the foundation of holidays, which is followed by the creation of coupling and procreation. Rebbi's arrangement of the first three orders mirrors this sequence exactly: Agricultural law, followed by Festival law, followed by Marital law. The words "*zera('im)*"[4] and "*moed*"[5]—the names of the first two Orders—are even mentioned in the narrative.

If the sequence of the first three orders of the Oral Torah is truly based on the Written Torah's account of creation, what justifies the arrangement of the last three orders? A close reading of the last verses in the creation story reveals an allusion to them, as well.

The Order of Tort law begins by listing the ox and pit as primary categories of destructive entities. That an individual can be held responsible for the havoc wrought by his animal and for damages engendered by his pit assumes that he is permitted to domesticate animals and excavate the earth in the first place. Such liberties should not be taken for granted. After all, "The earth is Hashem's, and everything in it, the world, and all who live in it."[6] The license to do so, therefore, must first be bestowed. And it is done so at the end of the sixth day of creation. Hashem, in the same breath commanding mankind to procreate, enjoins mankind to "fill the earth and subdue it, and rule over the fish of the sea and over the fowl of the sky and over all the beasts that tread upon the earth."[7] When mankind is commanded to subjugate the earth,

---

3   Ibid. 1:28.

4   Ibid. 1:11.

5   Ibid. 1:14.

6   *Tehillim* 24:1. Even if, perforce, mankind is allowed to till the soil and cultivate the land in order to eat, the license to dig the earth is not implied. See, for example, BT *Gittin* 47a, where a gentile who purchased the right to cultivate a plot in the Land of Israel still has no right to dig pits, ditches, and caverns. Indeed, even the basic right to eat of the earth's fruit, which is technically owned by Hashem, is not taken for granted in BT *Berachos* 35a.

7   *Bereishis* 1:28.

it is implicitly granted the license to dig pits, ditches, and caverns. Likewise, commanding mankind to subordinate the animals suggests domesticating and introducing them into human society. As a result, the need for Tort law is born.

Immediately after, however, Hashem limits mankind's grip over the animal kingdom. When Hashem gives man permission to eat of the earth's yield,[8] He limits his diet, forbidding him to kill and consume animal meat.[9] Yet, it is clear from the text later on that Hevel, Adam's son, does kill and sacrifice animals from his herd, an act pleasing to Hashem.[10] Adam, too, we are taught, brought animal sacrifices.[11] In light of the above decree, this practice is perplexing. Because of this difficulty, Rabbi Yaakov Ettlinger concludes that the inference excluding the killing of animals is limited to the harming of animals for food, but not for other uses such as clothing and sacrifices.[12] In other words, implied in the exclusion to kill and eat animals is the license to sacrifice animals, enhancing mankind's already robust dominion over the animal kingdom. Consequently, Rebbi, modelling his arrangement of the Oral Torah after the Written Torah's account of creation, follows Tort law with Sacrificial law.

Rebbi completes his organization of the Oral Torah with Purity law because that realm was created at the close of creation itself. In the final moments of the sixth day, Hashem looks at all He has made and finds it to be "very good."[13] It is said that, in the margins of his personal *Sefer Torah*, Rabbi Meir comments that Hashem's evaluation refers to the concept of death.[14] The prospect of death can be a strong motivational force to maximize one's limited time on this earth. With death and decay, however, comes contamination in all its varying degrees. The laws of purity regulate this metaphysical phenomenon.

---

8   Ibid. 1:29–30.
9   BT *Sanhedrin* 59b. Our sages infer that while man was given the earth's produce "to eat" (*Bereishis* 1:29), animals were excluded from his diet.
10   *Bereishis* 4:4.
11   BT *Avodah Zarah* 8a; *Rambam, Mishneh Torah*, Laws of the Temple 2:2.
12   *Aruch La'ner*, BT *Sanhedrin* ibid. Rabbi Reuven Margolis, in his work *Margaliyos Hayam* on *Sanhedrin*, goes so far as to say that for sacrificial purposes, the meat can even be eaten!
13   *Bereishis* 1:31.
14   *Bereishis Rabbah* 9.

To summarize, after distilling the entire corpus of the Oral Torah, which spans the ambit of the human experience, into six basic Orders, Rebbi patterns these Orders after the order of creation:

- On the third day, Hashem creates vegetation.
- On the fourth day, He creates the sun, moon, and stars.
- On the fifth and sixth day, Hashem fashions creatures and mankind, instructing them, respectively, to mate and procreate.
- Still on the sixth day, He grants mankind the license to harness—despite the attendant risk—both the earth and the animal kingdom for material and spiritual needs.
- At the conclusion of not only the sixth day but the entire endeavor, Hashem creates the reality of death.

In turn, Rebbi orders his masterpiece in the same succession:

1. Agricultural law (*Zera'im*)
2. Festival law (*Moed*)
3. Marital law (*Nashim*)
4. Tort law (*Nezikin*)
5. Sacrificial law (*Kodashim*)
6. Purity law (*Taharos*)

At this point, you may be asking yourself one of the following two questions:

1. Why does Rebbi, for his preeminent project, only see significance in the creation narrative from the third day and onward? What about the beginning of creation?
2. Even though Rebbi does begin his arrangement with Agricultural law (*Zera'im*), the first *masechta*, *Berachos*, doesn't address agricultural related laws until the sixth chapter, which concerns itself with classifying foodstuffs and determining the appropriate blessings for before and after eating. Instead, Rebbi's presentation of the Oral Torah actually begins with the laws of *Shema* and *tefillah*. How does the placement of these laws in Rebbi's sequence fit with the proposition that Rebbi's scheme corresponds to the creation narrative?

The truth is, however, that a close analysis of the very first Mishnah of *masechta Berachos* and its accompanying discussion in the Gemara—prompted and guided by the Mishnah's carefully chosen words—reveals that Rebbi's first concern is not the reading of the evening *Shema*, per se, but the establishment of when, precisely, the day ends and the night begins.

- According to halachah, does the night begin at sunset or when the stars come out?
- If the former, is the initial setting of the sun below the horizon considered "sunset," or is the reddening of the sky sometime later considered "sunset"?
- If the day ends when the stars come out, how many must be visible, and what size must they be to be significant?
- Alternatively, can a brief period preceding sunset—whenever that is—already be considered the onset of night?[15]

The answer to these questions dictates when the evening *Shema* can be recited.[16] Moreover, the Mishnah's treatment of the evening *Shema* before it considers the morning *Shema* points to another halachically significant assessment about the day-and-night cycle: the twenty-four-hour day begins with nighttime, followed by daytime.

What emerges is nothing less than startling. The very first Mishnah in the very first *masechta* in the very first Order of Rebbi's arrangement of the Oral Torah corresponds exactly to the very first utterances and to the very first creations made by Hashem on the very first day of creation: "G-d said, 'Let there be light,' and there was light. G-d saw that the light was good, and G-d separated the light and darkness. G-d called the light, 'day,' and the darkness, 'night.'"[17] Furthermore, because Rebbi discusses the evening *Shema* before the morning *Shema*, the Gemara immediately justifies this order of treatment by invoking the next line

---

15   This period is known as *plag ha'minchah*. According to Rabbi Yehudah, one can recite both the evening *Shema* and evening *tefillah* at this time.

16   BT *Berachos* 2a–b, with all its classic commentators.

17   *Bereishis* 1:3–4.

in the creation narrative, proving that daytime follows nighttime: "And there was evening and there was morning, one day."[18]

As ingenious as Rebbi's design is, his motive is still elusive. Why, indeed, does Rebbi systematically model the Oral Torah on Hashem's act of creation?

Perhaps we can suggest that Rebbi's design intends to underscore Hashem's ambitious agenda for us when He gifted us the Torah, both the Written and Oral. During the six days of creation, Hashem created the perfect physical, natural world; at Har Sinai, Hashem enjoined us to create the ideal human, social world. As Rabbi Joseph B. Soloveitchik writes in his magnum opus, *Halakhic Man*, mankind is obligated "to become a partner with the Almighty in the continuation and perfection of His creation...The perfection of creation, according to the view of halakhic man, is expressed in the actualization of the ideal Halakhah in the real world."[19] Just as Hashem created a finite physical world and implored man to develop it and unearth its vast material potential, so, too, Hashem authored the finite Written Torah and enjoined us—via the Oral Torah—to explicate its meaning and unleash its boundless moral and legal potential. By using the tools and teachings of the Oral Torah, we discover Hashem's value system and vision for our society: from an extensive and compassionate welfare system (*Zera'im*); to the mechanisms needed to shape a national identity and collective memory (*Moed*); to the regulated gender roles and family life necessary in order to enrich life and to perpetuate tradition (*Nashim*); to the establishment of a legal system that administers justice and protects society's most vulnerable (*Nezikin*); to the maintenance and management of a centralized

---

18   Ibid. 1:5; BT *Berachos* 2a. The laws of *tefillah*, too, serve as a backdrop for an analysis of the different parts of the day: When does the daytime begin—dawn or sunrise? How many parts is the morning comprised of? When does the morning end and afternoon begin? The answers to these questions determine when one can pray the morning, afternoon, and evening prayers, respectively. Rebbi's choice of *Shema* and *tefillah* as the subject matter to be used to reconstruct the phases of the day is consistent with his design. Once he models his sequence based on the creation narrative, it is only natural to frame the first discussion—the treatment of "day" and "night"—with a reference to the Creator Himself, to Whom we pray and Whose sovereignty we declare.

19   Rabbi Joseph B. Soloveitchik, *Halakhic Man* (JPS, 1983), pp. 105–7.

place of worship that inspires obedience and devotion (*Kodashim*); to the piety and awe-inducing rules of purity and contamination (*Taharos*).[20]

Our mandate, then, is twofold:

- First, we are enjoined to understand—through rigorous study— the Torah's singular philosophy and comprehensive moral system.
- Second, we are expected to implement those ideas and principles into practice in the real world.[21] Both steps are acts of creation. As Rabbi Soloveitchik says, "Halakhic man's approach begins with an [abstract] creation and concludes with a real one."[22]

Rebbi correlates his arrangement of the Oral Torah with the creation narrative found in the Written Torah both to reflect this lofty ambition and to inspire all future generations to live up to its calling.

With the help of Hashem, I have tried, over these past eight and a half years, to share Rebbi's vision with the members and *mispallelim* of Young Israel of Avenue J. Through *derashos* and *shiurim*, I sought to describe and demonstrate the nature of *talmud Torah* and its pursuit of an ideal culture.

This book, which is an adaptation of those discourses, intends to expose a wider audience not only to the brilliance and relevancy of the Torah but to its ambitious goal to shape society in its mold. For six days, Hashem created the world. Since then, He has granted us six millennia to complete what He started. The explosion and flourishing of *talmud Torah* in recent decades, throughout the world and especially in Israel, is a portent of things to come. The conceptualization and realization of the ideal Torah society, one that is to serve as a model for the rest of humanity, is just beyond the horizon. May we soon build it and behold it.

---

20 Ibid., p. 22. See also Rabbi Michael Rosensweig, "Reflections on the Conceptual Approach to Talmud Torah," in The Orthodox Forum series, *Lomdus: Conceptual Approach to Jewish Learning,* edited by Yosef Blau (MSYU, 1999), pp. 189–228.

21 *Halakhic Man,* pp. 17–21; Rabbi Shimshon Raphael Hirsch, *Nineteen Letters, Letter Eighteen,* in Joseph Elias, *The Nineteen Letters,* newly translated and with a comprehensive commentary (Feldheim Publishers, 1995), pp. 263–79; Rabbi Yechiel Yaakov Weinberg, "The Torah of Life, As Understood by Rav S.R. Hirsch," in *The World of Hirschian Teachings: An Anthology on the Hirsch Chumash and the Hashkafa of Rav Samson Raphael Hirsch,* (Feldheim Publishers, 2008), pp. 104–13.

22 *Halakhic Man,* p. 19.

Vayikra

Monotheism:
Why Is One Better Than Many?
Part I

I DO NOT recall what sparked the comment. It was a casual one, off-handed even. Sitting in class, in pursuit of a master's degree in social work at New York University, I was caught off-guard when my professor began to philosophize about religion. "What, really," he smugly asked, "is the difference between one god and many gods?" As far as he was concerned, a belief in any supernatural being, whether in one or in a variety, is both futile and infantile. The same sentiment led preeminent atheist, Richard Dawkins, to similarly remark, "It is not clear why the change from polytheism to monotheism should be assumed to be a self-evidently progressive improvement."[1] To be honest, even if I was

---

1   Richard Dawkins, *The God Delusion* (Boston: Mariner Books, 2006), p. 52.

prepared to retort, I wouldn't have; the last thing I wanted to do was to rub anyone, let alone a professor, the wrong way. I just wanted to fly under the radar and pass the course. Yet, even beyond the walls of the university, his remark tugged at my consciousness: Indeed, what *is* unique and progressive about the belief in one G-d over many? Why isn't the contemporary belief that there are no gods whatsoever the next logical and progressive step, as Dawkins and his ilk would have us to believe? After contemplating these questions for some time, if I would, by chance, meet my professor in the street, this is how I would respond to his seemingly nonchalant, yet intentionally provocative, remark. (It's amazing how much courage one can have when nothing is on the line.)

Reflecting on the presentation of the various sacrifices in *Sefer Vayikra*, our sages bring to our attention that the names of G-d, *E-l* or *Elokim*, are never used in connection with sacrifices. Instead, only His four-letter name, *Yud-Hei-Vav-Hei*, articulated reverentially as "Hashem" (literally, "The Name"), is used.[2] Never one to overlook subtle shifts in terminology himself, the *Ramban* observes that throughout the Flood narrative (especially when G-d first appears to Noach, informs him of the impending doom, instructs him to build an ark, and assures him that he and his immediate family, along with one pair of every animal species will be saved), the Divine name of *Elokim* is used. Only when G-d beckons Noach to enter the ark and to bring seven pairs of pure animals along with one pair of every impure animal does the four-letter name, "Hashem," appear in the text. This is so, explains the *Ramban*, because at this point in the saga, Hashem hints to Noach that he will be offering sacrifices upon exiting the ark,[3] and sacrifices are associated only with the name Hashem, not *Elokim*.[4]

---

2   BT *Menachos* 110a, in the name of Rabbi Shimon ben Azzai. See also *Sifri* 143 for a slightly different version.

3   By instructing him to bring seven pairs of pure animals fit for sacrifice.

4   *Ramban, Bereishis* 7:1. The *Ramban* references his broader treatment of this issue in his commentary to *Vayikra* 1:9, where he quotes the Gemara cited above as the origin of this dichotomy.

It is well-known that the name Elokim captures G-d's strong sense of justice, while the name Hashem represents His compassion.[5] This distinction, however, is not enough to explain the exclusive usage of the name Hashem in the context of sacrificial rites, as both attributes of G-d, justice and compassion, are at play. Instead, our sages explain that the name Hashem is used exclusively at the expense of E-l and Elokim "so as not to give a claim to a litigant to argue."[6] *Rashi* interprets the Gemara to mean that if different names of G-d were associated with the various sacrifices, one could mistakenly claim that, in fact, different gods were being worshipped! To preclude this possibility, the Torah sticks to one name—Hashem.[7]

This interpretation, though, is difficult for two reasons:

- First, even the uninitiated knows that G-d has multiple names. If the Torah's multifaceted presentation of G-d throughout the Torah doesn't pose a theological problem, why should there be a particular concern in the context of sacrifices?
- Moreover, even if we do grant that the area of sacrifices has a certain vulnerability not found elsewhere, *Rashi*'s approach doesn't explain why, of all the Divine names, the name Hashem was singled out to provide consistency and avoid misunderstanding.

Perhaps we can suggest an alternative interpretation behind the Torah's concern that using the names E-l and Elokim (instead of, or along with, the name Hashem in the contexts of sacrifices) would give an antagonist the upper hand.

Rabbi Yehudah HaLevi, in his book, *Kuzari*, distinguishes between the divine names Elokim and Hashem as follows. The word *elohim* is the plural form of *el*, which means a force or power. For this reason, anyone in a position of authority, such as a ruler or judge, can be called an *el*. Polytheists would identify various perceived forces in their lives and worship each one in hope of garnering favorable outcomes. Since polytheists worshipped an array of forces, the collection was called

---

5   See, for example, *Rashi, Bereishis* 1:1.
6   BT *Menachos* ibid.
7   *Rashi*, BT *Menachos* ibid.

elohim. The designation *elohim*, then, is a generic term used to refer to the power these imagined gods wield. Since G-d is Omnipotent and Sovereign of all, He is appropriately called *Elokim*. The name Hashem, on the other hand, used by monotheists, is a proper name of G-d. As one would call his friend "Reuven" or "Shimon," G-d is called "Hashem," and like a true proper name, the name Hashem "captures" G-d's "personality," so to speak.[8]

The different ways polytheists and monotheists relate to their respective god(s) is not merely superficial; how one refers to his or her god reflects the nature and terms of their relationship. The polytheist, who refers to his gods as forces, sees his gods as something to be manipulated and used for self-serving purposes. The world is both a frightful one filled with dangers and a bountiful one offering much pleasure. Primitive man, driven by his basic drives of survival and gratification, is preoccupied with satisfying his desires and avoiding premature death. Confronted with elements that seem to control these outcomes, it is only natural for primitive man to attempt to sway these forces in his favor in any way he can, especially when doing so doesn't restrict his urges.

As such, the polytheist's relationship with his gods is neither meaningful nor mutual. It is not meaningful because the gods are merely a means to the polytheist's ends; it is not mutual because the relationship is overwhelmingly one-sided. The worshipper places his demands and expects results from his gods without any genuine concern for the will of his respective gods or commitment on his part other than having to perfunctorily perform certain prescribed rituals.

The monotheist's relationship with G-d, however, is both meaningful and mutual. The monotheist, who refers to his G-d by His proper name, is not indifferent to G-d's interests and does not perceive G-d as merely a tool to be manipulated, as a means to some greater personal ends. Instead, the monotheist and Hashem have entered into a long-term relationship whereby each party has rights and responsibilities, where

---

8   *Kuzari* 4:1.

there are mutual expectations, and where there is mutual respect for the dignity of the other. The monotheist was not enticed to enter into this relationship for primitive reasons; after all, in this arrangement his urges are regulated, not gratified. Rather, he is motivated to serve Hashem because he perceives the rightness of Hashem's expectations of him. That G-d is also referred to as *Elokim* by the monotheist doesn't belie this characterization of their relationship; rather, it is an honest acknowledgement of Hashem's abilities and sovereignty.[9]

The development from polytheism to monotheism is a significant improvement because it reflects mankind's psychological and moral maturation. While the polytheist is primitive, the monotheist is progressive.

Because the shift from polytheism to monotheism is a function of psychological and moral growth, it is no surprise that it is painstakingly achieved, its process replete with setbacks. No event in Jewish history illustrates this more than the sin of the Golden Calf. Having miscalculated how long Moshe Rabbeinu was supposed to be away on Har Sinai, the people panic and, with the aid of Aharon, fashion a golden calf, which they begin to worship. According to the *Ramban*, B'nei Yisrael never intended to *replace* Hashem and worship a foreign god. Instead, they sought to *represent* Hashem with the golden calf. Conditioned in Egypt to worshipping tangible, visible gods, their inability to see or touch Hashem haunted the people, something they were able to handle only as long as Moshe stood in for Hashem. Without Moshe—and out of a desperate need for security—they fashioned the golden calf to stand in for Hashem.[10]

Support can be brought from the text demonstrating that B'nei Yisrael, at the time, were not mature enough to embrace an abstract, morally demanding G-d and worship Him in the context of a mutual relationship. When the people crowd around Aharon to act, they demand from him an "*Elokim*."[11] And when the golden calf is finally fashioned,

---

9   See, for example, *Rashi, Bereishis* 2:4, where the Torah refers to G-d as "Hashem, *Elokim*."
10   *Ramban, Shemos* 32:1.
11   *Shemos* 32:1.

they point to it and declare, "This is your *Elokim*, O' Israel, that took you out of Egypt."[12]

To the fledgling nation that just emerged from centuries immersed in a polytheistic culture, G-d was not a being with a personality and preferences but a mighty force that had saved them from its oppressors. Like the *elohim* of Egypt, which were represented by icons, animals, and people, B'nei Yisrael demanded a tangible object to represent their Savior, their newfound *Elokim*.

This insight into the psyche of the people may shed light on why Aharon fails to dissuade them, and, instead, becomes implicated in their sin. Each Shabbos, a *haftarah*, a passage from Navi that is usually thematically similar to the weekly Torah portion, is read. Consequently, the *haftarah* for *Parashas Ki Tisa*, where the episode of the golden calf is recorded, is the dramatic confrontation between Eliyahu HaNavi and the idolatrous prophets of Ba'al.[13] In the days of Eliyahu, the Jewish People's polytheistic tendencies got the best of them once again, as it did at the foot of Har Sinai. Our sages, however, selected a similar passage in Navi not only to compare the two readings but to contrast the two readings, often as a critique on a particular Biblical figure.[14] In our case, this is quite clear. Unlike the episode in the *parashah*, which ends in tragedy, the *haftarah* ends in triumph. The contrast is startling:

- What does Aharon do wrong that results in his and the people's disgrace?[15]
- What does Eliyahu do right that leads to the people's whole-hearted return to G-d?

After he fashions the golden calf—but before the people dance around it and worship it—Aharon tries to redirect the masses away from the idol and toward G-d. In a last effort to get the people to worship G-d directly, without the medium of the golden calf, Aharon builds a *mizbei'ach*

---

12   Ibid. 32:4.
13   *Melachim I* 18:1–39.
14   I am indebted to Dr. Yehudi Felman for exposing me to this approach to *haftaros*.
15   For Aharon's disgrace, see *Shemos* 32:35 and *Devarim* 9:20. See also BT *Sanhedrin* 7a.

and proclaims, "A festival for Hashem tomorrow!"[16] Alas, it is to no avail. The next day, the masses, in revelry, sacrifice to the golden calf. Aharon fails because he misses what the masses need to hear. Although they have no choice but to worship the one and only G-d, they aren't ready to relate to Him as Hashem—to serve G-d altruistically simply because it's the right thing to do. Only weeks removed from their Egyptian masters' polytheistic culture, the people are only capable of relating to G-d as Elokim, as a power that can provide them safety and security. Aharon fails because, when they ask him for an *elohim*, he offers them Hashem. When Aharon needs to be realistic, he is too idealistic.

It's almost as if Eliyahu, standing on Har Carmel, is conscious of Aharon's grave error when he challenges the prophets of Ba'al in the presence of the people. Eliyahu calls for two bulls and declares:

> *Let Ba'al's prophets choose one for themselves, and let them cut it into pieces and put it on the wood, but not set fire to it. I will prepare the other bull and put it on the wood but not set fire to it. Then you call in the name of your Elokim, and I will call in the Name of Hashem. The Elokim who answers by fire—He is Elokim.*[17]

Immediately, the people eagerly respond, "What you say is good."[18] Because Eliyahu is aware that the masses have relapsed and have come to see worship as a self-serving tool used to manipulate the powerful gods to act in their favor, he frames his appeal to the one true G-d in those terms—Elokim—while, at the same time, referring to Him by His proper Name, Hashem. And when he implores G-d to send a Heavenly fire to consume his bull, Eliyahu cries, "Answer me, Hashem, answer me, so these people will know that You, Hashem, are Elokim, and that You are turning their hearts back again."[19] Once again, by addressing Hashem as the Elokim, Eliyahu indicates that he knows that the

---

16 *Shemos* 32:5.
17 *Melachim I* 18:23–24.
18 Ibid. 18:24.
19 Ibid. 18:37.

masses—in order for them to come to his side—must be assured that the god they choose to worship is all-powerful and capable of granting their needs of posterity and prosperity. On cue, when Hashem sends down a fire and it consumes Eliyahu's bull, the people lose themselves and shout, "Hashem—He is Elokim! Hashem—He is Elokim!"[20] Had Aharon been more attuned to the people's psychological state and had he framed his call to celebrate before Hashem in a way that would have appealed to the people's primitive needs, history may have been different. B'nei Yisrael might have abandoned the golden calf and worshipped Hashem, the Elokim, directly.

By this point, it should be clear that monotheism can resemble polytheism. In other words, there are two types of monotheists:

1. The moral monotheist—who sees Hashem as a Being who has dignity and serves Him because it is the right and good thing to do.
2. The primitive monotheist—who sees Elokim as a means to his own ends and serves Him to garner favor, i.e., in the hope that he will be granted health and wealth.[21]

Qualitatively speaking, the latter type is not so different from the polytheist. Although one serves many gods and the other only one, both worship for base and self-serving reasons. To be sure, the primitive monotheist is superior, acceptable even, as long as he refrains from worshipping G-d in unauthorized ways, such as through idols. Yet, his form of worship is relatively immature, somewhat inauthentic, and far from the ideal.

It is for this reason that only the name Hashem is used in the context of sacrifices, never E-l or Elokim. Throughout, the Torah refers to G-d as E-l or Elokim, as well as by His other names, because, as we mentioned above, these names accurately reflect certain attributes of G-d.

---

20 Ibid. 18:39.
21 The idea that there are fundamentally two types of monotheists that can be understood in these terms is borrowed from Rabbi Joseph Soloveitchik in *Halakhic Man*. He refers to them as *halakhic man* and *homo religiosus*. When our sages referred to "one who serves G-d out of love" and "one who serves G-d out of fear," they may have meant this as well.

If, however, we were commanded to bring offerings in order to appease Elokim, monotheism could be misconstrued as nothing more than a delusion to satisfy our primitive needs and as a belief system that demands nothing more than to find favor before the supposed Almighty. Moreover, framing monotheistic worship in terms of polytheism would only stunt our psychological and moral growth, encourage our primitive tendencies, and nurture our predisposition toward polytheism and idolatry. As long as we see G-d only in terms of a Force and are drawn to Him because of His power, we are susceptible to substituting other perceived forces to worship in order to curry favor, instead of or alongside Him.[22]

In order "not to give a claim to a litigant to argue," and to preempt any antagonist, such as Richard Dawkins or my NYU professor, from misunderstanding moral monotheism and conflating it with primitive polytheism, the Torah exclusively uses G-d's proper Name, Hashem, to underscore that our worship of Him is within the context of a meaningful and mutual relationship, and that we are expected to serve Him, not for primitive reasons, but for moral ones.

---

22   See Rabbi Shmuel Eidels, in his commentary *Maharsha* to *Menachos* 110a, who has a similar but different formulation of this second point.

Tzav

Monotheism:
Why Is One Better Than Many?
Part II

ACCORDING TO THE *Rambam*, the entire institution of sacrifices is a concession to human weakness. Knowing man's psyche, Hashem could not realistically expect B'nei Yisrael to immediately abandon the forms of Divine service that they were used to. Surrounded for centuries by pagan worship in Egypt, which consisted of animal offerings, incense burning, and wine libations, a call to serve Hashem without these rituals would be incomprehensible and appear too foreign to them to be accepted. Instead, Hashem "compromised" and provided the familiar framework within which the people could comfortably worship Him exclusively.[1]

---

1   *Moreh Nevuchim* 3:32.

The non-essential nature of sacrifices, says the *Rambam*, is the subtext of the constant refrain heard from the prophets that Hashem is not interested in our many offerings but in our loyalty to Him.[2] It is also the deeper meaning behind Yirmiyahu's questionable recollection of early Jewish history: "From when I freed your fathers from the land of Egypt, I did not speak with them or command them concerning burnt offerings or sacrifice. But this is what I commanded them: Do My bidding, that I may be your G-d and you may be My people; walk only in the way that I enjoin you, that it may go well with you."[3] How can Yirmiyahu claim that Hashem did *not* command our forefathers regarding sacrifices when a plethora of mitzvos regulate sacrificial rites?

The *Rambam* explains that, indeed, the first mitzvos given to B'nei Yisrael in the wake of the Exodus did *not* concern sacrifices at all; instead, the first set of mitzvos addressed the fundamental principles of truth and justice, embodied in the laws of Shabbos and civil law, respectively. This prioritization highlights the Torah's value system. Even when the subject of sacrifices was finally broached, and extensively so, the institution was only of secondary importance, its function being to wean B'nei Yisrael off of idolatry and serve as a necessary means to realize the primary focus of the Torah: to listen to His voice, to identify as Hashem's people, and to serve Him exclusively, forgetting forever the ideas of idolatry. Tragically, the people in Yirmiyhau's day confused the means with the ends.[4]

The *Ramban*, however, forcefully argues with this theory.[5] In his view, the institution of sacrifices has inherent spiritual significance and is a central feature of the worship of Hashem, irrespective of what B'nei Yisrael were or weren't used to. After all, the Torah repeatedly describes offerings as a "pleasant aroma to Hashem,"[6] a characterization not compatible with any scheme that sees sacrifices as a mere concession, a necessary evil. Beside for their mystical effect, sacrifices carry weighty

---

2   *Shmuel I* 15:22; *Yeshayahu* 1:11.
3   *Yirmiyahu* 7:22–23.
4   The *Rambam* there, and in 3:46, addresses the exception of *Korban Pesach*.
5   *Ramban, Vayikra* 1:1.
6   *Vayikra* 1:9, 13, 17, 6:8, 14.

symbolism, expressing, for example, our utter submission to Hashem and willingness to sacrifice ourselves in recognition of our sins.[7]

The *Meshech Chochmah* attempts to reconcile these two diametrically opposed views. He suggests:

- The *Ramban's* positive assessment of the value of sacrifices is correct, in general.
- The dispensation to offer sacrifices on private altars, known as *bamot*, which was granted to B'nei Yisrael periodically, was indeed a concession to their idolatrous leanings, as per the *Rambam's* explanation.

During short intervals, when there was no central place to pay homage to Hashem in the land of Israel, the Torah was concerned that the masses, scattered throughout the land, would succumb to their deep need for security and a sense of control over their fate and offer sacrifices to the sundry deities of the indigenous people. *Bamot*, therefore, were reluctantly sanctioned to curb this urge and enable the people to offer instead their hopes and fears to Hashem. Because this practice was not ideal but a necessary evil, sacrifices brought on *bamot* are not considered a "pleasant aroma to Hashem."[8] This is the *Meshech Chochmah's* explanation.

Perhaps we can suggest a different synthesis of these two conflicting views, one that not only gives more prominence to the *Rambam's* perspective but results in a more comprehensive theory of the sacrificial institution than the one proposed by the *Meshech Chochma* in his reconciliation. As mentioned in our earlier discussion of the relationship between polytheism and monotheism, polytheism and pagan worship are not arbitrary, irrational systems of thought. They are reasonable, albeit immature and immoral, responses to basic human needs of security and satisfaction. For our current discussion, the main point is this: these primitive drives are part of the human condition, and the

---

7   According to the *Ramban*, Yirmiyahu was rebuking the people not for confusing priorities, but for their hypocrisy and duplicity.

8   Commentary to *Vayakira* 1:1; see also BT *Zevachim* 113a.

subconscious mind, which subtly and secretly influences our thoughts and actions to satisfy these base needs, is universal, too.

So, when the *Rambam* posits that Hashem provided sacrificial rituals in anticipation of B'nei Yisrael's vulnerability to polytheism and idolatry, we can appreciate this insight. Not only because B'nei Yisrael, in particular, had historically been exposed to it as slaves in Egypt, but because the inclination toward idolatry is part of the human condition, applying to all peoples at all times. As we encountered in our previous discussion, even when an individual or a society is committed to the One True G-d, the tendency exists to relate to G-d not as Hashem, with Whom to have a relationship, but only as an *Elokim*, as a means to achieve self-interested ends.

If, as we are suggesting, polytheistic leanings are an inherent and immutable part of human nature, which threatens to undermine monotheism, then it is not only conceivable but expected that the Torah would address this essential problem in a realistic and prudent way by accommodating and "channeling" this human flaw in some manner. Yet, it does not necessarily follow that, just because sacrifices, incense offerings, and libations were adopted and adapted by polytheists, they have no intrinsic value as modes of legitimate Divine worship. We can, therefore, propose that both the *Rambam* and *Ramban* are correct: the Torah promotes an extensive sacrificial system for the dual purpose of conceding to human nature and to provide a highly significant form of worship.

One place where the Torah attempts to achieve its dual objective—to wean B'nei Yisrael away from outright polytheism and to afford the nation with an ideal mode of monotheistic worship that is not corrupted by polytheistic ideologies and tendencies—is the prohibition of *shechutei chutz*, sacrificing offerings outside the confines of the *Mishkan* or Beis Hamikdash. Remarkably, the Torah focuses on this prohibition not once but twice: first in *Sefer Vayikra* and then again in *Sefer Devarim*. Why the two renditions? Based on our analysis, we can suggest that the dual treatment corresponds to the dual aspect of the sacrificial system:

- *Sefer Vayikra* highlights the aspect of accommodation, and addresses the primitive human inclination to serve multiple gods and forces.
- *Sefer Devarim* emphasizes the inherent meaning and ideal nature of the sacrificial system, and addresses the primitive human inclination to serve G-d, not as Hashem, but as an *Elokim*.

Sefer Vayikra, which relates to B'nei Yisrael as they travel in the wilderness, proscribes them from offering sacrifices "on the open field,"[9] insisting instead that they bring their offerings to the *Mishkan* so that "they shall no longer slaughter their offerings to the demons after whom they stray."[10] *Sefer Vayikra* guards against the universal human tendency to seek solace and a sense of control among the many perceived forces that exist in the world—from demons to deities.

Sefer Devarim, however, which addresses a more mature nation on the verge of entering, conquering, and cultivating the Land of Israel, juxtaposes the ways of the indigenous polytheistic nations who worship their gods "on high mountains and on hills, and under every leafy tree"[11] with monotheistic practice: "You shall not do this to Hashem, your G-d. Rather, only at the place that Hashem, your G-d, will choose…to place His Name, there shall you seek out His Presence and come there."[12] *Sefer Devarim* intends to preclude the primitive monotheist, who conflates monotheism and polytheism, sees G-d only in terms of *Elokim*, and serves Him only with the hope that he will be granted health and wealth in return. To correct this behavior, the Torah forcefully contrasts itself from the ways and philosophies of polytheism. A system of thought that appeals to perceived higher powers for self-serving reasons takes it for granted that these gods will be easily accessible when and wherever the worshipper needs. The whole appeal of polytheism is that it implicitly inverts the relationship between the worshippers and worshipped, making the former's demands primary. Similarly, a corrupted monotheism,

---

9   *Vayikra* 17:5.
10   Ibid. 17:7.
11   *Devarim* 12:2.
12   Ibid. 12:4–5.

which resembles polytheism in its orientation, would conceive of its one and only *Elokim* to be available when and wherever He is wanted. To dispel B'nei Yisrael of this potential misconception of monotheism, the Torah demands of the people to come and worship Hashem exclusively in the place He chooses, and beckons them "to seek" Hashem there and develop a meaningful relationship with Him.

Because polytheistic leanings are a function of the human condition, they are difficult to control. However, with proper instruction and patience, these natural propensities can be subdued, albeit with much adversity and setbacks. This process is reflected in the presentation of the two renditions of *shechutei chutz* in the Torah. That the first treatment of the prohibition is placed in the earlier *sefer* of *Vayikra* and the second one in the later *sefer* of *Devarim* is not merely a matter of chronology. The presentation reflects a development—a transition from addressing the more primitive polytheistic manifestations (to serve multiple gods and forces) to its more advanced manifestations (to serve G-d not as Hashem, but as an *Elokim*) as the nation matures.

Every time a *navi* rebukes the people for overemphasizing sacrificial rites at the expense of moral and ethical behavior, it indicates a setback, as the people's distorted priorities betray their true motives: to use G-d as a means to their ends. Ultimately, the Torah expects B'nei Yisrael to fully mature, tame its polytheistic tendencies, and embrace G-d once and for all as Hashem. As *Hoshea* envisions:

> *And it shall be on that day!—the word of Hashem—that you will call Me Ishi (my husband), and you will no longer call Me Ba'ali (my master). I will remove the names of Ba'alim (Masters) from her mouth and they will not be mentioned again by their name.*[13]

The *navi* foresees a time when B'nei Yisrael will no longer have the psychological need for a *master* to whom to serve, not a pagan *Ba'al* nor a monotheistic *Elokim*. Instead, as a reflection of the nation's full

---

13   *Hoshea* 2:18–19.

development, they will only want a *husband*, with whom they can share a mutual and meaningful relationship.[14] Their mature need will, of course, be reciprocated. As they are promised: "I will betroth you to Me forever; and I will betroth you to Me with righteousness, with justice, with kindness and with mercy; and I will betroth you to Me with fidelity, and you will know Hashem."[15]

---

14   See *Malbim* ibid., who interprets the thrust of the verse and phrase *"Ba'alim"* this way too.
15   *Hoshea* 2:21–22.

Shemini

Deliverance and Disgust

THE TORAH CONCLUDES its extensive treatment forbidding abominable and impure species by justifying these restrictions: "For I am Hashem Who brings you up from the land of Egypt to be a G-d unto you."[1] For some reason, the Torah deviates from its usual formula when referring to Hashem taking us out from Egypt. Elsewhere, G-d is described as the One "Who took you *out (hotzeisicha)*."[2] Here, however, G-d is portrayed as the One "Who brings you *up (hamaaleh)*." This subtle difference was not lost on our sages:

> *It was taught in the Academy of Rabbi Yishmael that the verse means to say: "Had I not brought Israel out of Egypt for any reason other than that they do not make themselves impure*

---

1   *Vayikra* 11:45.
2   For example, see *Shemos* 20:2.

through creeping things as do the other nations, dayam"—it
would have been a sufficient cause for them to have been re-
deemed, and abstaining from creeping things is an elevation
for them. This is why the Torah here uses the expression
"bring up."[3]

Although this explanation satisfies the textual discrepancy we
started with, it now leaves us even more perplexed. If Hashem would
have taken us out of Egypt just to prohibit creeping creatures, *dayeinu*
(it would have been enough for us)!? In what way does refraining from
eating them justify—by itself—our redemption from bondage? Why is
the prohibition of creeping creatures given such moral prominence and
spiritual standing?

In his book, *The Anatomy of Disgust*, William Ian Miller, professor of
law at the University of Michigan, observes that beyond the language
of Right and Wrong, the language of Disgust is also used to navigate
our moral world. The visceral and verbal reactions of disgust that we
all experience when confronted with that which repulses us extend to
moral circumstances as much as it does to material ones. Not only does
the idiom of disgust ("gross," "nasty," "repellent," "nauseating," etc.)
exist alongside the lexicon of "right and wrong" and "good and evil," it
is, according to Miller, more potent. Unlike the language of Right and
Wrong, which merely reflects our moral convictions, the language of
Disgust strengthens them. Disgust, says Miller, is unique in this way
for three reasons:

1. Disgust is intuitive.
2. Disgust is concrete.
3. Disgust is objective.

Let us explore these three ideas:

- Disgust is intuitive—The feeling of disgust is immediately understood without needing to be proved or justified. The sense of
  revulsion aroused by that which disgusts is taken for granted by

---

us as something that is non-negotiable. As Miller elegantly puts it, "when a norm is backed by disgust, we are in its grip."[4] There is a difference, therefore, between norms we merely accept and ones that are unshakable. "Norms we accept are maintained by talk and discussion, by debating and reasoning, while those which have us in their grip simply come to dominate our wills,"[5] which leaves no room for compromise. Whether or not a norm is perceived as something that is simply accepted by us or has us in its grip often depends on the emotion and language we use when we witness or partake in its violation. Feelings of guilt and condemnation in terms of right and wrong indicate acceptance; feelings of sickness and censure in terms of disgust marks that we are in the norm's grip.[6]

- Disgust is concrete—"By being so much in the gut, the idiom of disgust has certain virtues voicing moral assertions. It signals seriousness, commitment, indisputability, presentness, and reality. It drags the moral down from the skies toward which it often tends to float, wrests it from philosophers and theologians, and brings it back to us with a vengeance. The day-to-day nitty gritty of moral decision, moral policing, moral education, and morality talk is more likely to involve reference to the disgusting than to the Good and the Right."[7] Being repulsed by an offense makes the underlying moral principle less intellectual. Instead of talking abstractly of what is right or wrong, the emotion of disgust gives us vivid words, such as nasty, ugly, abominable, and gross, which makes talking about morals more down to earth and readily understood, felt even.

- Disgust is objective—When someone else is disgusted, we know exactly how they feel. With other emotions, however, such as sadness or hopefulness, it is much harder to grasp the precise

---

4   William Ian Miller, *The Anatomy of Disgust* (Harvard University Press, 1997), p. 201.
5   Ibid.
6   Ibid.
7   Ibid., p. 180.

quality of the feeling that the other is experiencing. Disgust, by contrast, is readily identifiable. As Miller observes, "Disgust poses less of a problem for intersubjectivity than perhaps any other emotion. When you say you love or that you feel regret, I am never quite sure of your inner state in the way I am when you say you are disgusted…When you have the creeps or feel defiled I know what is going on inside you. Disgust thus communicates rather better than most emotions."[8] Because the feeling of disgust is easily recognized by the community, the idiom of disgust is a powerful way to convey moral disapproval.

We were redeemed from Egypt with a mandate: to serve as an exemplar for all of humanity. As the blueprint for this ideal community, with its distinct set of conventions, the Torah's foremost concern is finding ways to guarantee the preservation of its morals and mores. What better way to do so than to introduce the idiom of disgust into its legal narrative, leveraging disgust's unique set of attributes—that it is intuitive, concrete, and objective—to shape and strengthen its adherents' convictions. The Torah, therefore, seizes the opportunity to incorporate the idiom of disgust into its lexicon in the legal passage where it most naturally fits: creeping creatures and impure animals. The entire passage prohibiting creeping creatures and impure species is replete with the idiom of disgust: "*sheketz hu*"—it is abominable. "*Sheketz hu*" grabs the reader and grips the audience like no legal jargon can. The message is crystal clear: Eating forbidden creatures is not just wrong, it is disgusting. By extension, all of the Torah's prohibitions should not be viewed simply as norms we dutifully accept but as behaviors that are offensive and conflict with our sensitivities. At times, the Torah will even borrow the language of disgust to shape our moral sensibilities. For example, we should avoid bringing idols into our homes not only because they are theologically problematic but because they are objects we should "loathe"[9] and "abominate."[10] Since the passage of creeping

---

8   Ibid., p. 194.
9   *Devarim* 7:26.
10   Ibid.

creatures provides us with a graphic language to promote and preserve our unique culture, had Hashem not redeemed us from Egypt for any reason other than to forbid disgusting creeping things, *dayeinu*.

The success of the Torah's usage of the idiom of disgust to shape and strengthen our moral convictions is captured in the following midrash about Rabbi Akiva:

> *When Rabbi Akiva went to Rome, he was informed upon to a certain magistrate, who sent him two beautiful women, bathed, anointed, and adorned like brides, and they pressed themselves upon him throughout the night. The one saying, "Come to me," and the other saying, "Come to me," and he sat between them spitting, and turned to neither. In the morning, they left and went to see the magistrate, and said to him, "We would rather die than be given to this man." He sent for him. He said to him: "Why did you not do with these women what men are wont to do with women? Are they not beautiful? Are they not human like you? Did He who created you not create them as well?" He said to him: "What could I do? Their smell came over me [as if] from the flesh of carcasses, mortally injured animals, and creeping things."[11]*

It is no coincidence that Rabbi Akiva expresses his revulsion in terms of forbidden meat and creeping creatures, for it is this very passage where the Torah integrates the idiom of disgust into our moral world. The magistrate's attempts to appeal to Rabbi Akiva's reason, to debate him analytically, are useless. Rabbi Akiva doesn't merely accept the Torah's ethic, which would make him susceptible to discourse; he is gripped by it. The notion of promiscuity disgusts him; the prostitutes themselves nauseate him. No argument in the world can convince him otherwise.[12]

---

11   *Avos D'Rabi Nosson* 16:2.

12   Our approach to the religious significance of disgust, in general, and Rabbi Akiva's revulsion, in particular, are compatible with the teaching of Rabbi Elazar ben Azaryah, quoted in Rashi (*Vayikra* 20:26), which states: "A person should not say, 'I am nauseated by pork' or 'I do not

The *Navi* Malachi chastises the people for disrespectfully bringing inferior animals as offerings. Hashem, the *navi* informs us, asks incredulously, "You bring the stolen and the lame and the sick [animal], and bring it as an offering—shall I accept it from your hand?"[13] Remarkably, Hashem considers a stolen animal as unfit as one that is deformed or sickly. By conflating the otherwise healthy animal with physically repulsive ones, Hashem Himself utilizes the idiom of disgust to express his revulsion of stolen property. He does so in the hope that disgust's unique set of attributes—that it is intuitive, concrete, and objective—will seize, shape, and shift the moral compass of his chosen people.

---

wish to wear clothes made of wool and linen.' Rather, he should say, 'I wish to eat pork and wear the forbidden mixture, but what can I do? My Father Who is in Heaven has decreed upon me not to.'" Rabbi Elazar ben Azaryah is talking about a *natural* revulsion; Rabbi Akiva's is a *cultivated* revulsion. Indeed, obedience should not be the result of a predisposition that a person happens to already have. Instead, obedience should be an expression of submission to Hashem. The highest form of submission, though, is the remaking of one's personality and sensibilities in accordance with Hashem's will. A similar approach can be found in Rabbi Eliyahu Dessler's *Michtav Me'Eliyahu* (volume 1, p. 117), where he discusses the increasing levels of mastery of free choice (*bechirah chafshis*).

13   *Malachi* 1:13.

Tazria-Metzora

Too Comfortable
in One's Own Skin

ONE HUNDRED and twenty years before the Flood, Hashem commands Noach to begin building the ark.[1] Noach is told its specific dimensions, which materials to use, precisely how many floors it should have, and that it is to be comprised of numerous and various compartments.[2] The Hebrew word used for compartments is "*kinim*," the same word for the plural form of a bird's nest.[3] Because of this association, our sages infer that Hashem was insinuating to Noach:

---

1   See *Bereishis* 6:3 with *Rashi*'s commentary.
2   *Bereishis Rabbah* 31:9. See also *Rashi*, *Bereishis* 6:14.
3   The singular form is *kan* when the word is *tafel*, such as in the phrase "*kan tzippor*"; the singular form is *ken* when the word is used alone.

Just like a pair of birds is used to purify the *metzora*, so, too, your ark will purify you.[4] The questions, of course, abound:

1. Why is Noach instructed to commence constructing the ark one hundred and twenty years prior to the Flood? As intricate a design the ark may have been, the assembly couldn't possibly have demanded so much time.
2. Why does Noach need purification? In what way is he tainted?
3. What is the connection between a *metzora*, his sin, and his purification process with the building of the ark?

Although we commonly associate *tzaraas* with a kind of abnormal skin condition,[5] the metaphysical malady can manifest in two other ways, as well: on one's clothing,[6] and on the walls of one's house.[7] Why are these three areas specifically singled out to host *tzaraas*? What is the common denominator between them? Let us turn to our sages' reflections on indifference in the face of communal suffering to resolve our inquiry:

> *When the community is in trouble, a person should not say, "I will go to my house, and I will eat and drink, and all will be well with me." Rather, a person should share in the distress of the community. Perhaps a person will say, "Who is there to testify against me?" The very stones of his house and its beams testify against him. As it states in Chavakuk, "For a stone will cry from the wall and a small piece will answer it from the beams."*[8] [9]

At first glance, it would seem that our sages are merely informing the would-be intransigent that, contrary to his assumption, he is, in fact, under constant watch and his misdeeds will not evade detection.

---

4   *Bereishis Rabbah* 31:9. In Rabbinic Hebrew, a *ken* is a pair of birds. Thus, the tractate that discusses different scenarios and their outcomes when pairs of sanctified birds get mixed up with one another is called *Kinim*.

5   *Vayikra* 13:1.

6   Ibid. 13:47.

7   Ibid. 14:34.

8   *Chavakuk* 2:11.

9   BT *Taanis* 11a.

However, there is a deeper message being conveyed: it is the very walls, the very protection and privacy that his house provides that breeds his indifference.

Indeed, safety, modesty, and moments of solitude are indispensable values, but there is an inherent social risk when we erect walls to secure them. In an effort to physically separate ourselves from the outside world due to perceived threats, we can become psychologically detached from those we never meant to exclude. This unintended consequence is not limited to the walls of our homes. We wear clothing to protect us and to preserve our dignity. Our skin, too, shields us against microbes and the elements, and, through the sensations of pain and itch, signals the brain when it detects danger lurking on the body. For this reason, skin is metaphorically described in the Torah as a garment, as in "You clothed me with skin and flesh."[10] As with one's house or clothing, an individual can overly identify with his skin. As Primo Levi once said, "I live in my house as I live inside my skin: I know more beautiful, more ample, more sturdy, and more picturesque skins; but it would seem to me unnatural to exchange them for mine." Any of these useful barriers can, gradually, engender an antisocial attitude.

It is well known that *tzaraas* is an affliction that develops as a result of speaking *lashon hara*. Yet, more often than not, slander is not spoken maliciously but as a result of dissociation, where the offender doesn't even perceive what he is doing as wrong. His skin, clothing, and house have isolated him to such a degree that he has lost touch with basic social dynamics and etiquette. No longer can he anticipate the potential damage caused by his casual speech, no longer is he concerned with what transpires outside the confines of his home, clothing, and skin.

Social incompetence and indifference, however, do not only manifest themselves in slander; they can also produce the very opposite: silence. We have already discussed at length elsewhere[11] that Noach's major flaw was his failure to influence his generation. Unlike Avraham Avinu,

---

10   *Iyov* 10:11.
11   *A Time to Seek*, pp. 17–24.

who speaks up on behalf of the wicked people of Sodom,[12] Noach makes no effort to impact his culture. To the contrary, Noach isolates himself from the ills of society.[13] Because he has no personal initiative, Hashem is compelled to intervene:

> *There is much relief and salvation before G-d. Why, then, did He trouble Noach with this construction? So that the people of the Generation of the Flood should see him busy with the ark for a hundred and twenty years and ask him, "Of what use is this to you?" Noach would say to them, "In the future, the Holy One, Blessed is He, is going to bring a flood upon the world." Thus, through the construction of the ark, they might repent.*[14]

The simple understanding of this midrash is that Hashem has Noach build the ark for an extended period of time in order to intrigue the people, inform them of their impending doom, and give them an opportunity to repent. According to Rabbi Baruch Yitzchak Yissacher Leventhal, however, the focus was less about raising the people's moral awareness than about heightening Noach's social conscience. Like the *metzora*, who needs guidance to recognize, contemplate, and atone for his sin of slander, Noach needs assistance to recognize, contemplate, and rectify his sin of silence. By turning the construction of the ark into an ongoing spectacle, Hashem forces Noach to engage with his generation.[15]

Perhaps we can add that the building of the ark with all its compartments (*kinim*), which not only protected its passengers from the raging waters but provided privacy from each other, adds another dimension to Noach's education. As we have seen, means of protection and privacy often result in the unintended consequence of indifference to the circumstances of others, which can lead to socially irresponsible slander

---

12   *Bereishis* 18:23–32.

13   *Zohar* I:58b (Pitzker edition, 2004); Rabbi Shimshon Raphael Hirsch, commentary to *Bereishis* 6:10.

14   *Tanchuma* 5 and *Bereishis Rabbah* 30:7, quoted in *Rashi, Bereishis* 6:14.

15   R. Leventhal, *Birkas Yitzchak*, p. 10.

or silence. The purifying ritual (consisting of *kinim*) that the *metzora* undergoes, and the compartments (*kinim*) that Noach must build, both intend to communicate that erecting necessary barriers should not inhibit social sensibilities and responsibilities.

Henry David Thoreau, American writer and philosopher, is best known for his book, *Walden*, a reflection upon his experience living in an idyllic, rural setting for more than two years. Thoreau was keenly aware of the unintended social and spiritual consequences of living in a large, densely populated commercial city and needed a respite. To get away from the excess materialism and isolating nature of city life, he sought temporary refuge in the natural surroundings of Walden Pond in Concord, Massachusetts. Thoreau, though, never abandoned his permanent residence, and his retreats helped him maintain a healthy, balanced perspective. He once said of his home in the city, "I had three chairs in my house: one for solitude, two for friendship, three for society."

Often, we are compelled to build all kinds of walls to protect ourselves and our families from the adverse influences of our surrounding culture. At the same time, it behooves us to guard against the temptations of insularity. Over time, social isolation not only engenders social ineptitude and indifference but undermines our *relevance* in a world we are destined to shape. Our lifestyles, instead, should be balanced, with our homes containing three chairs: one for solitude, two for friendship, three for society.

Acharei Mos

Kisui Ha'dam: A Moral Cover-Up?

ALTHOUGH RITUAL SLAUGHTER (*shechitah*) applies to all kosher animals indiscriminately, the mitzvah of *kisui ha'dam*, the commandment to subsequently cover the blood that is spilled, only applies to birds and wild animals, not to domesticated animals. Why? Our sages justify the scope of the mitzvah as follows:

> *After murdering his brother, Hevel, Kayin is unsure what to do with the corpse cast down on the ground before him. By way of instruction, Hashem stages a fight between two birds, whereupon one kills the other and then proceeds to dig and bury the carcass. Witnessing the altercation and its aftermath, Kayin digs a grave and buries Hevel. Because of their role in Kayin's*

education, the birds merit that their blood will be covered after
every ritual slaughter.[1]

A slightly different version of the episode depicts not Kayin but a variety of birds and wild animals tending to Hevel's burial. For their efforts, two blessings will be recited over them: one when they are ritually slaughtered and another when their blood is subsequently covered.[2] Although these accounts are meant to clarify why *kisui ha'dam* applies only to birds and wild animals—and not to domesticated animals—the substantive connection between the burial of Hevel and the mitzvah to cover up the blood of ritually slaughtered animals is elusive. What does one have to do with the other? How does the midrash achieve its objective to explain, in any meaningful way, why *kisui ha'dam* excludes domesticated animals?

One factor of the narrative we have yet to explore is Kayin's indecisiveness. Why does he need to be shown the way by the wildlife? Although Kayin may not have been able to intuit the moral demand for a proper burial, the need to at least cover or hide the body in order to conceal his wrongdoing is quite obvious.[3] Why, then, was Kayin paralyzed by the sight of his brother's corpse lying untouched on the ground? As we will see, perhaps Kayin was immobilized by a dilemma that many murderers face, and one that ultimately prevents another fratricide, much later on in history, from occurring. The dilemma that grips Kayin only after he kills Hevel gives Yosef's older brothers pause and leads them to spare his life.

After seizing Yosef and throwing him into a pit to await his eventual execution, his brothers notice a caravan coming their way. Seeing an alternative solution to murder, Yehudah convinces his brothers to sell Yosef instead. After all, he says, "What gain will there be if we kill our brother and cover up his blood?"[4] Yet, the gain is obvious. They would rid themselves of their brazen, threatening brother. Because of this problem, *Rashi* renders Yehudah's argument in terms of monetary gain, "What financial gain would we accrue by killing our brother and

---

1   *Tanchuma* 10.
2   *Bereishis Rabbah* 22:8.
3   Indeed, other midrashic accounts envision Kayin hiding the body in the bush.
4   *Bereishis* 37:26.

concealing his death?"[5] The *Chizkuni*, however, offers the following interpretation of Yehuda's appeal:

> *If we murder our brother, we will not be able to glorify in it, for we would be compelled to cover up the crime and conceal his death because of the pain the truth would cause our father. And when a person avenges himself against his enemy, there is no satisfaction if he cannot glorify in it.*[6]

The brothers, in Yehudah's view, were in a bind. Not only did they want to kill Yosef, they craved to exalt in their triumph over his perceived treachery. If, however, they would be forced to conceal Yosef's demise—"to cover up his blood"—in order to avoid suffering guilt over the agony they would have caused their father, their drastic deed would be ungratifying, essentially for naught. Without a way to glorify in Yosef's death, the brothers reconciled themselves to only being able to remove him permanently by unglamorously selling him away.

In the same vein, but tragically after the fact, Kayin is conflicted:

- On the one hand, Kayin wants to leave Hevel's corpse lying out in the open to glorify and revel in his victory over his Divinely favored brother.
- On the other hand, he cannot escape the nagging guilt over what he has done, to Hevel, to his parents, and to his family. So, he also wants to suppress the ill-feeling, cover up his crime, and conceal the evidence.

Kayin, too, is ambivalent about "covering up his brother's blood." Paralyzed by his dilemma, Kayin does not know which course to take. That is, until the wildlife gets involved. The reason our sages portray the birds and wild animals showing Kayin the proper way of burial and resolving his conflict is because every time we hunt, trap, and slaughter a bird or wild animal, we struggle with a moral conflict, which is resolved by "covering its blood with earth."[7]

---

5   *Rashi* ibid.
6   *Chizkuni, Bereishis* ibid.
7   This is a slight paraphrase of *Vayikra* 17:13.

Our interaction with domesticated animals is uncomplicated. A simple trade-off frames our relationship: in exchange for nurturing and shepherding them on our farms, plains, and pastures, we enjoy their wool, milk, and even meat. This arrangement is peaceful. Domesticated animals are not our prey, they are our partners. Within this framework, our humanity is never in question. Our relative superiority is never in doubt. The only safeguard necessary against potential abuse is ritual slaughter, whereby we consider the value of each animal, one at a time, and take its life swiftly and painlessly.[8]

When we set out, however, to "hunt down prey, beast or bird,"[9] we encounter a multifaceted dilemma:

- On the one hand, all animals, including wild animals and birds, have been placed under our stewardship and control to be used as we see fit.[10]
- On the other hand, unlike with domesticated animals, we have neither entered into a mutual relationship with the wild animal and bird, nor integrated them into our society. Instead, to obtain their hide and meat, we must leave civilization and hunt them on their own turf, an arena where there is no reciprocity and no mercy. As a result, we have anxiety about what we are doing. First, are we right for preying on them? Perhaps we should feel guilty about exploiting their inferiority. Moreover, by preying on them the way they are preyed on by carnivorous beasts, are we at risk of becoming bestial too? Will hunting and trapping and killing and eating them condition us to become cruel and uncivilized?

In order to resolve our anxieties when we hunt game, we are commanded not only to kill it through ritual slaughter but to partially "cover [the blood] with earth."[11] The latter ritual reconciles our moral conflict as follows:

---

8   See *Sefer Hachinuch* 451.
9   *Vayikra* 17:13.
10   *Bereishis* 1:28.
11   *Vayikra* 17:13. See BT *Chullin* 88a and *Shulchan Aruch, Yoreh Deah* 28:15, which states that one need not cover all of the blood.

- By superficially concealing the blood of the animal or bird we had captured in the wild, we give expression to our ambivalence regarding outsmarting and killing an animal we had no prior, reciprocal relationship with. By doing so, we lessen the force of our moral misgivings and make the killing more psychologically bearable.

- By considerately covering the blood of the animal or bird we had preyed upon, we symbolically distance ourselves from the animal kingdom and preclude our primitive urge to gloat over our kill. Acting in a respectful manner toward the dead animal demonstrates our humanity, despite our initial aggressiveness.[12]

Although in a civilized society murder is never sanctioned, the killing of animals is endorsed. Yet, the taking of any life is a violent act. Consequently, protections against abuse and cruelty must be put into place. Since the nature of our relationship with different types of animals varies, our protective measures are nuanced, as well. Because the killing of domesticated animals does not elicit any guilt or engender any images of one animal preying on another, *shechitah* suffices to define the killing as a humane act. Killing wild animals and birds, however, is particularly vexing, inviting both guilt and comparisons between us and predatory animals. Accordingly, the mitzvah of *shechitah* is augmented by the mitzvah of *kisui ha'dam* to mitigate our moral uneasiness and preserve our humanity.[13]

---

12   Although our sages (BT *Chullin* 84a and *Toras Kohanim* 7:11) derive exegetically that *kisui ha'dam* applies to domesticated birds, such as geese and chickens, as well as to an already trapped bird or wild animal one acquires, the Torah intentionally presents all scenarios in terms of "hunting prey." Because of their elusive and liberated nature, our experience killing birds and wild animals, however we ultimately come to do so, is conceptually defined as "hunting prey."

13   There is much evidence that *kisui ha'dam* is not a distinct mitzvah but is, conceptually, an extension of *shechitah*. However, an analysis of the debate amongst the early commentators concerning how to conceptualize the mitzvah is beyond the scope of this work. For the interested reader, see, for example, *Rashi*, BT *Beitzah* 7b, s.v. *Ha lo kashya*; *Ran, Chullin* 28b (found in the folio of the *Rif*), d"h *U'modeh Rabbi Yehudah l'inyan berachah*; and *Avi Ezri*, commentary to *Mishneh Torah*, Laws of Shechitah 14:1.

Kedoshim

The Peshat and Derash of Chukim and Mishpatim

IT IS COMMONLY assumed that the set of mitzvos classified by the Torah as *"chukim"* are laws that are inexplicable. This common understanding of *chukim* has been heavily influenced by *Rashi*, who throughout his commentary to the Torah consistently defines *chukim* as the laws of Hashem, "which have no rationale."[1] Whether the phrase appears before[2] or after[3] the giving of the Torah, *Rashi*, almost without fail, renders *chukim* as laws without any comprehensible reason, whose nature incites the Evil Inclination, Satan, and the gentile nations to provoke us and question, "Why are they legislated?" and "Why do we

---

1   *Rashi, Vayikra* 19:19.
2   *Bereishis* 26:5; *Shemos* 15:26.
3   *Bamidbar* 19:2; *Vayikra* 18:4.

41

have to observe them?" *Rashi*'s interpretation is informed by our sages, who sharply contrast the laws categorized as *mishpatim* and *chukim*:

> *"You shall do My ordinances (mishpatim), and you shall keep My statutes (chukim) to follow them, I am the Lord your G-d."*[4] *My ordinances (mishpatim) is a reference to matters that, even had they not been written, it would have been logical that they be written. They are the prohibitions against idol worship, prohibited sexual relations, bloodshed, theft, and blessing G-d, a euphemism for cursing the Name of G-d.*
>
> *The phrase: And you shall keep my statutes (chukim), is a reference to matters that Satan and the nations of the world challenge because the reason for these mitzvos are not known. They are: The prohibitions against eating pork; wearing garments that are made from diverse kinds of material, i.e., wool and linen; performing the chalitzah ceremony with a yevamah, a widow who must participate in a levirate marriage or chalitzah; the purification ceremony of the leper; and the scapegoat of Yom Kippur. And lest you say these are meaningless acts, therefore the verse states: "I am Hashem,"[5] to indicate: I am Hashem, I decreed these statutes and you have no right to question them.*[6]

We can suggest, however, that this dichotomy is misleading. We will demonstrate, on the one hand, that *chukim* do have a rationale and, on the other hand, that *mishpatim*, while intelligible, are not a set of natural laws that are universally appreciated. To reconcile this approach with *Rashi*'s view and the comments of our sages, we offer that there are two levels of interpretation for the terms *chukim and mishpatim*: *peshat* (plain-sense meaning) and *derash* (derived meaning):

- According to *peshat*, *chukim* and *mishpatim* have similar meanings, and are often even synonymous.

---

4   *Vayikra* 18:4.
5   Ibid.
6   BT *Yoma* 67b, *Sifra* 13:9 to *Vayikra* 18:4.

- It is only on a *derash* level that a conceptual chasm separates *chukim* and *mishpatim*.

The strongest proof that *chukim*, on a *peshat* level, connotes laws that are indeed comprehensible is the passage in *Sefer Devarim*, where Moshe encourages the nation to remain loyal to Hashem and to take pride in their unique heritage:

> See, I have imparted to you chukim and mishpatim, as Hashem, my G-d, has commanded me, for you to abide by in the land that you are about to enter and occupy. Observe them faithfully, for that will be proof of your wisdom and discernment to other peoples, who on hearing of all these chukim will say, "Surely, that great nation is a wise and discerning people." For what great nation is there that has a god so close at hand as is Hashem, our G-d, whenever we call upon Him? Or what great nation has chukim and mishpatim as perfect as all this Teaching that I set before you this day?[7]

If *chukim* were laws with no rationale and were objects of ridicule that tested our loyalty to Hashem, Moshe's address is very difficult to understand.[8] According to Moshe, the opposite is true: our *chukim* (and *mishpatim*) are objects of admiration and will induce profound respect among the gentile nations. Far from being incomprehensible, the wisdom and righteousness reflected in our *chukim* are discernable and will be envied. Moshe's speech is coherent precisely because the plain-sense meaning of the phrase *chukim* is laws that have underlying reasons.

This *peshat* interpretation of *chukim* is also evident from its usage in the Torah before the mitzvos were ever given. For example, Hashem justifies the blessings coming to Yitzchak Avinu and his descendants "because Avraham obeyed My voice and observed My safeguards, My commandments, My *chukim*, and My teachings."[9] *Rashi*, as expected, interprets the text in light of the opinion found among our sages that

7   *Devarim* 4:5–8.
8   The *Kli Yakar* to *Bamidbar* 19:2 also asks this question.
9   *Bereishis* 26:5.

Avraham Avinu observed all of the six hundred and thirteen mitzvos, and understands that these various phrases refer to different categories of mitzvos. According to *Rashi*, while "My commandments" refer to the comprehensible *mishpatim*, "My *chukim*" refer to the mitzvos that have no intelligible reason and that are derided by the Evil Inclination and gentile nations. The *Ramban*, however, after quoting and analyzing the opinion of our sages and *Rashi*, offers the "plain-sense"[10] interpretation, which accords with what we know about Abraham from elsewhere in the Written Torah. In this scheme, these various categories of worship refer to Avraham's belief in G-d, his campaign against idolatry, and his fulfillment of anything G-d had commanded him, including circumcision, in particular. According to *peshat*, "My *chukim*" refers to Avraham's "following the ways of Hashem, being gracious and merciful, and performing kindness and justice for others."[11] For the *Ramban*, on a *peshat* level of interpretation, *chukim* is synonymous with *mishpatim*.

Likewise, when the Torah records that, soon after the splitting of the sea, while the nation was camped in Marah, Hashem "established for the nation a decree (*chok*) and an ordinance (*mishpat*),"[12] the *Ramban* interprets on a "*peshat*"[13] level that *chukim* and *mishpatim* are defined as reasonable and prudent laws. Both refer not to specific mitzvos from the list of six hundred and thirteen, as *Rashi* interprets, but to principles and practices that would regulate the nation's behavior while they travel through the desert. Similarly, says the *Ramban*, when Yehoshua, in his farewell address, "made a covenant with the people that day and set down decrees ("*chok*") and laws ("*mishpat*") for them in Shechem,"[14] he wasn't emphasizing certain mitzvos of the Torah, but rather had instituted "standard practices and by-laws regulating the orderly and amicable settlement of society."[15]

---

10   In his commentary to ibid.
11   Ibid.
12   *Shemos* 15:25.
13   *Ramban, Shemos* 15:25.
14   *Yehoshua* 24:25.
15   *Ramban* ibid. *Ramban* also brings prooftexts that "*chok*" connotes any set practice. For example, "Allot me my daily [*chuki*] bread" (*Mishlei* 30:8), and "Had I not set up the fixed patterns

The *Ramban* addresses *Rashi*'s interpretation of *chukim* directly and observes that our sages never said that *chukim* have *no* rationale; rather, their emphasis was that, unlike *mishpatim*, *chukim* are subject to derision and doubtfulness. Moreover, it is inconceivable to say that certain mitzvos have no underlying reason because we have a tradition that "every word of G-d is purifying."[16] This implies that all mitzvos, *chukim* included, are purposeful and designed to refine both human character and society.[17]

What, then, is the difference between *mishpatim* and *chukim*? The Written and Oral Torah do treat them as separate categories of mitzvos. The *Ramban* asserts that, though both are comprehensible, the reasons for the *mishpatim* are readily apparent to even the uninitiated, while the rationales behind the *chukim* can only be discerned by the educated elite:

> *Chukim are matters that are "edicts of the king," an "edict" being a matter that is conceived by the king, who is the one with the most wisdom concerning governing the kingdom, and he is the only one who knows the full extent of the need and benefit of that order that he commands, and he does not relate the reason to the people of his kingdom, except to the wisest of his advisors[18]...and since the masses are unaware of the rationale, they do not find them satisfying, rather, they question the need for them in their hearts, while accepting them in practice out of fear of the government. So, too, the chukim of the Holy One, Blessed is He, are the esoteric laws that He has put in the Torah, which the masses, in their minds, do not find satisfying as they do the mishpatim. In truth, however, all the laws have a sound rationale and absolute benefit.[19]*

[chukos] of heaven and earth" *Yirmiyahu* 33:25. See also *Shemos* 12:43, where *chok* refers to the set of laws regulating the *Korban Pesach*. For a list and analysis of the decrees instituted by Yehoshua, see BT *Bava Kama* 80b–81a.

16   *Mishlei* 30:5.
17   *Ramban*, *Vayikra* 19:19.
18   Ibid. 18:6.
19   Ibid. 19:19.

According to the *Ramban*, through rigorous study, the meaning behind the *chukim*, their place in the Torah's overall value system, and
their contribution to furthering man's and society's development is
recognizable. Once elucidated by scholars, the *chukim* then become
accessible to many others, even if there will always be a class of people
who will continue to question their integrity, because they still cannot
appreciate their nuances and complexities.

Having demonstrated that *chukim*, on a *peshat* level, *do* have underlying reasons that are comprehensible, we can now turn our attention to
mishpatim and show that, on a *peshat* level, these are not universal laws
that could have been formulated by anybody, anywhere. First, while the
general thrust of many *mishpatim* are easily understood and could have
been independently formulated, their respective details—and there are
many—are nuanced and reflect a deeper insight into the human condition and the needs of a complex society that the average person would
not anticipate independently or even appreciate once elucidated.[20]

Even more fundamentally, the reason that *mishpatim*, on a *peshat*
level, cannot be defined as universal is that the whole notion is based
on a misconception: that there is something called "common sense."
The concept of common sense is, by definition, a set of practices that
is not a result of judgment or interpretation, but is so because it is so.
However, the whole idea is a misnomer. Any law, custom, or habit of
any given culture is based on assumptions. It is precisely because these
assumptions are taken for granted, their truth and rightness unassailable and unspoken, that for insiders to act or think otherwise would go
against "common sense." Yet, these assumptions are often not shared
by other cultures, and the logic or reasonableness of these behaviors
is not at all apparent to outsiders![21] For example, the custom found
in some cultures to stand up for an uncle, a brother of one's mother,
is only commonsensical if one assumes that both matrilineal family

---

20   Rabbi Shimshon Raphael Hirsch, *Nineteen Letters, Letter Eighteen*, in Joseph Elias, *The
     Nineteen Letters*, newly translated and with a comprehensive commentary (Feldheim
     Publishers, 1995), p. 158.

21   Clifford Geertz, *Common Sense as a Cultural System.*

ties are significant and that an uncle is an authority figure. Even if the concepts of honor and family are widely understood, if any of the above assumptions are not shared by an outsider, the gesture of honor shown to a maternal uncle would seem foolish, if not irrational. Even the prohibitions of murder and theft are not obvious. Only if one assumes that humans have a dignity that distinguishes them from the animal kingdom would someone automatically articulate a law against murder or theft. Otherwise, a culture could assume that survival of the fittest is a basic principle, which would inform a whole different set of norms and shape an alternate "common sense."

Not only does common sense differ from culture to culture horizontally, it varies vertically, too. Meaning, the same society may, over time, develop a new set of values and assumptions, which, in turn, produce a different, updated "common sense." We can illustrate this phenomenon with the attitude toward honoring one's parents. Everyone in *Rashi*'s school of thought places honoring parents not in the *chukim* category, but in the *mishpatim* one.[22] Yet, there are contemporary societies that do not take honoring one's parents for granted, as something that is "common sense." Not too long ago, a woman who had left her rent-controlled apartment for an indefinite period of time to go overseas to care for her dying mother was at risk of losing her apartment. The judge decided in her favor and justified his decision with the following reflection:

> *There was a time in many cultures when the care of a sick or elderly parent by a child was the hallmark of familial responsibility. But, according to that frequently uttered refrain, times change. Mothers or fathers, sometimes both, would often live under the same roof with their offspring and the hands-on care provided would be substantial. To the outsider, considerable sacrifice seemed involved, but for the caregiver child, the care*

---

22   See, for example, *Netziv, Shemos* 20:12. *Maharal, Gur Aryeh, Devarim* 5:16, actually thinks honoring parents is more universal and basic than even *mishpatim*, classifying it in a different category called "*teva*," instinctive laws.

of mom and dad was the natural progression in life's journey;
those who reared and raised, and gave life, would be comforted
and looked after in the twilight of their own.

Sad to say, as with so many old-fashioned values, adherence
dims with each new generation, and parental care in some
instances has been reduced to an occasional call to a nurse's
aide or an infrequent, obligatory visit to a nursing home. But
there are those, undoubtedly dwindling in number who remain
students of the old school, staying true to basic traditions. The
tenant in our case is one of those rare individuals, and her
heartfelt decision to travel to Greece to be at her mother's side
during a final illness should not visit upon her the draconian
penalty of forfeiture of her long-held regulated apartment.

These remarks are a sad commentary on the changing values and
assumptions of many contemporary cultures: sacrifice has been supplanted by selfishness, tradition by trends, authority by autonomy, and
a sense of continuity by conceit. A culture that takes the former values
for granted sees honoring one's parents as "common sense." A culture
that embraces the latter set of values perceives honoring parents as
backwards and bizarre. Moreover, this judicial opinion illustrates vividly that *mishpatim* are readily comprehended and easily anticipated
only by those who take for granted their underlying assumptions and
value system.

After having outlined the two schools of thought regarding *chukim*
and *mishpatim*, it is important to realize that we need both interpretations, both the *peshat* and the *derash*. We need both the *derash*-driven
classification of mitzvos that preserves *Rashi*'s dichotomy between
chukim and *mishpatim*,[23] as well as the *peshat* based scheme that, like
the *Ramban*, treats *chukim* like *mishpatim* as a set of comprehensible,
meaningful laws.[24] The *derash* of *chukim* and *mishpatim* conditions us
to observe all of Hashem's commandments unconditionally, whether

---

23   *Maharal* ibid.
24   Rabbi Shimshon Raphael Hirsch, *The Nineteen Letters*, no. 10 and 11.

we grasp them or not, whether we are inspired or not, whether we are admired or ridiculed. The *peshat* of *chukim* and *mishpatim* protects the Torah from being reduced to a set of commandments composed of universal laws redundantly codified, comprehensible ceremonies based solely on Jewish history, and a host of irrational rules and rituals. The *peshat* of *chukim* and *mishpatim* enhances our prestige, as we are the only people privy to a comprehensive system of thought and practice that is predicated on an unmatched insight into theology, psychology, sociology, economic theory, ethics, and political philosophy, everything needed to properly shape character and mold a society that is stable and just. The *peshat* of *chukim* and *mishpatim* challenges us to immerse ourselves in Torah study, to locate, identify, and articulate its unique set of values and morals, and to cultivate a Torah personality that is animated by these discoveries.

Emor

Peace in Our Time

SHORTLY AFTER HIS wife gave birth to their son, the following humorous conversation took place between the new father, Shalom, a Secular Humanist, and his more traditional Jewish mother:

> *"What's his name?"*
>
> *"Paix."*
>
> *"Max?"*
>
> *"Paix."*
>
> *"What kind of name is Paix?"*
>
> *"It means 'peace.' Like my name but without the G-d bit."*
>
> *"Why would you name your kid 'peace'?"*
>
> *"What?"*
>
> *"Who names their kid 'peace'?"*
>
> *"You named your kid 'peace.'"*

"I named my kid 'peace'? Who did I name 'peace'?"

"Me. You named me 'peace.'"

"I didn't name you 'peace.'…"

"My name means 'peace,' Mom."

"Yeah, but that's not why we named you it."

Like all secular humanists, Shalom believes he can be good without G-d. Lofty goals, such as justice, compassion, and peace can be realized by mankind without having to turn to a higher source for instruction; our intellect is more than enough to know how to live humanely. As modern as it may sound, this sentiment is not new. While it does not appear explicitly, secular humanism does find expression in the Torah—in the unlikely personality of a mother whose pursuit of "peace without the G-d bit" ends in tragedy, with the death of her son.

It's the first time the Jewish nation executes someone. During one of the many encampments along their journey in the desert, one unnamed man, the son of an Egyptian man and Jewish woman, becomes embroiled in a heated argument with a native Jew. As the conflict escalates, the former becomes verbally abusive and blasphemes G-d. The consequence for such an egregious offense is dire, and the perpetrator is stoned to death by the entire congregation in accordance with Torah law.[1] Who is this unnamed man? Other than the fact that his father is Egyptian, the only identifying information we know is the name of his Jewish mother: Shelomis bas Divri.[2] Yet, that is all we need to know in order to reconstruct the episode and to trace the blasphemer's circumstances of birth and its role in his fateful confrontation that leads to his demise.

Without parallel in the annals of human history, despite being a people enslaved in Egypt for centuries, no Jewess, as a result of righteousness and modesty, was ever sexually involved with her oppressors. Well, except for one.[3] Shelomis bas Divri. She was impregnated by an

---

1   *Vayikra* 24:10–23.
2   Ibid. 24:11.
3   *Rashi* ibid.

Egyptian taskmaster. Generally speaking, the Torah considers a rape victim to be without fault, as blameless and helpless as a murder victim.[4] In this specific case, however, and without diminishing the culpability and criminality of the perpetrator, the Torah does not find the victim to be entirely blameless. The Torah does not see a moral contradiction between, on the one hand, unequivocally condemning an aggressor, and, on the other hand, weighing a victim's liability for any risk taken that factually enabled the assault. Shelomis bas Divri, flouting Jewish standards of modesty, draws undue attention to herself by being excessively friendly. As her name indicates,[5] "she was a chatterbox. She would speak with everybody. She would chatter to individuals, "Peace unto you," and to groups, "Peace unto you." Chattering with words, inquiring after everyone's welfare. This is why she found herself in a morally compromising situation."[6] Mistaking her gregariousness as an elicitation for something more, the Egyptian taskmaster is aroused and, subsequently, abuses her. Years later, the product of that devastating encounter finds himself without a Jewish father and excluded from any tribal affiliation. Feeling socially isolated and rejected, he acts out against both a native Jew and G-d Himself.

Both the Torah and secular humanism strive for peace. These two systems of thought, however, drastically differ in how to define the concept of peace. Shelomis bas Divri, in deed and in name, encapsulates what can transpire when one embraces the secular humanist concept of "peace without the G-d bit." According to the Torah, peace is not to be achieved at all costs, coming at the expense of other values and virtues. The Torah's vision of societal peace, called *Shalom*, is a product of many principles, including chastity and modesty. Although somewhat inhibiting, these virtues promote peace by nurturing mutual respect and regulating hostile primitive tendencies.

---

4   *Devarim* 22:26.
5   *Shelomis* is a derivative of the word *Shalom*, peace. *Divri* is formed from the word *Dibur*, speech.
6   *Rashi* ibid.

Deviating from these guidelines, Shelomis bas Divri practices her own version of peace that she thinks is humane. Ultimately, her indiscriminate friendliness, intended to promote peace, invites violence. That her form of peace is devoid of godliness is reflected in her full name. Her name is not purely Shelomis—a derivative of *Shalom*, a peace defined by Divine virtues; rather, her name Shelomis is qualified by *bas Divri*—her peace is the derivative of Speech and Sociability. Her definition of peace is stripped of Divine input, is secular in nature, and is a function of permissiveness and promiscuity.

Our sages teach us, "An uneducated person cannot be pious."[7] Why not? Without the Torah as our guide, we have no external criteria by which to measure our accepted definitions of noble concepts, such as peace, justice, compassion, and dignity. Peace and justice and compassion and dignity "without the G-d bit" become nothing more than what we want them to be. In the best situation, our biased, misguided definitions imperceptibly and gradually result in social and moral decay. In the worst situation, immediate and manifest evil is garbed in these noble concepts, shackling law-abiding and peace-loving citizens from taking any corrective action.

Uncertain of how to please Hashem, the *navi* Michah reminds the people: "He has told you, O' man, what is good, and what Hashem demands of you; but to do justice, to love kindness, and to walk discreetly with your G-d."[8] Only Hashem can tell us how to be good—what the parameters of peace and justice and compassion and dignity are. To try to define them otherwise, on our own, is not progressive but regressive.

---

7   *Pirkei Avos* 2:5.

8   *Michah* 6:8.

Behar

Making Sense Out of Servanthood

THE INSTITUTION OF the *eved Ivri* (Jewish bondsman) is highly protected, and for good reason. Because, as a servant, the *eved Ivri* is quite vulnerable, the Torah legislates many internal safeguards to prevent any exploitation:

- To preclude any confusion between an *eved Ivri* and a slave, the Torah prohibits the purchase of an *eved Ivri* in the marketplace[1] and explicitly warns his master, "You shall not work him with slave labor"[2] and "Do not subjugate him through hard labor."[3]
- The Torah emphasizes that the *eved Ivri* is, legally, like a hired worker, not a slave, and should be treated accordingly.[4]

---

1   *Vayikra* 25:42.
2   Ibid. 25:39.
3   Ibid. 25:43.
4   Moreover, our sages teach (BT *Kiddushin* 20a) that "anyone who acquires an *eved Ivri* is

- For this reason, an *eved Ivri* goes free automatically after a mere six years of service, and even earlier if he can procure the funds to redeem himself on a prorated basis.[5] A slave, on the other hand, who is enslaved indefinitely, would have to pay his total market-value to acquire his freedom.

However, if the institution of *eved Ivri* is inherently susceptible to abuse, why does the Torah permit purchasing an *eved Ivri* at all? Instead of vigilantly guarding it, wouldn't abolishing the entire institution be more prudent and serve society better?

This problem is compounded when we consider that, besides for the ethical dangers, the institution poses theological difficulties. Treating an *eved Ivri* as if he were a slave belies who his true master is: Hashem. The Torah stresses more than once that to treat an *eved Ivri* like a slave is unconscionable, "for they are My slaves, whom I have taken out of the land of Egypt."[6] It is a mistake to think that Hashem liberated us from bondage in Egypt to be free; rather, Hashem redeemed us and became our new Master. Enslaving another Jew ignores Hashem's pre-existing ownership. Acutely aware that the institution of the *eved Ivri* represents a threat to His rights, Hashem only redeems us from Egypt on condition that we will always free our Jewish bondsmen at the end of six years of servitude.[7] Rather than condition our freedom on our compliance with the laws regulating the institution of *eved Ivri*, why doesn't Hashem just do away with it entirely?

Our sages teach us that Hashem created the world in ten utterances.[8] Based on the thought of the *Maharal*, Rabbi Yitzchak Hutner explains that, by creating the world in ten phases instead of all at once, Hashem symbolically affirms the idea of hierarchy. Had Hashem created the world with only one utterance, He would have conveyed that all

---

considered like one who acquires a master for himself" because he must be careful to treat his *eved Ivri* at least as good as he treats himself.

5   *Shemos* 21:2, 8.

6   *Vayikra* 25:42.

7   *Yirmiyahu* 34:13–14; JT *Rosh Hashanah* 3:5 finds an allusion to this stipulation in *Shemos* 6:13.

8   *Avos* 5:1.

creations share the same stature and that, likewise, society should be organized in an egalitarian fashion. Instead, by using ten utterances, one after the other, Hashem divided creation into varying categories of significance, justifying and inviting human society to be arranged with hierarchies as well.

Hashem chooses the latter scheme because it best serves the purpose of creation: for all to admire and honor Him.[9] The gesture of lifting one's eyes toward a higher rank is the essence of paying respect, as it acknowledges the greater significance of the other. In an egalitarian system, there can be no proper conception of admiration or honor. Where everyone has equal stature, who would be the object of one's admiration? Upon whom would one bestow honor? When sameness is vigilantly guarded and all differences are summarily dismissed as not being fundamental—when everyone is to exist on the same plane—there is no one to look up to. This is not just a sociological issue; it is also a theological matter. In a system in which no one ever considers to lift one's eyes upward toward an ideal that seems beyond one's reach, people are not conditioned to properly relate to a G-d deserving of our admiration and expressions of honor. However, a society that is structured by divisions and is delineated according to varying personal status does nurture admiration and honor. Hierarchies imply varying degrees of stature and encourage looking upwards and paying respects—not only to fellow humans of greater stature but to G-d Himself.[10]

Hashem's design for society to be organized by hierarchy is challenged by Korach. Notwithstanding any hidden agendas, Korach disputes the authority of Moshe and Aharon and advocates for egalitarianism so that all Jews will be treated equally, without any one individual having more power, prestige, or privilege than another. Korach justifies his rebellion on the claim that "the entire congregation, all of them, are holy."[11] To demonstrate publicly and unequivocally that Korach is wrong, Moshe proposes a competition of sorts, through which "in the

---

9   *Yeshayahu* 43:7; BT *Kesubos* 8a.

10   *Pachad Yitzchak, Shavuos* 8:2.

11   *Bamidbar* 16:3.

morning, Hashem will make known those who belong to him."[12] Our sages wonder why Moshe stresses the time of day, and suggest that the phrase "in the morning" alludes to a logical flaw in Korach's argument:

> *Moshe said, "The Holy One, Blessed is He, has distinguished boundaries in His world. Can you confuse morning with evening? And that is what is written in the beginning, 'There was evening and there was morning.'[13] And it is stated, 'G-d separated the light and the darkness'[14] for its use in the world. And just as He made a separation between the light and the darkness, so did He separate Israel from the nations, as it is stated, 'I have separated you from the [other] peoples to be Mine.'[15] So also did He separate Aharon, as it is stated, 'Aharon was separated to consecrate the most holy things.'[16] If you can confuse this distinction in which He made a separation between the day and the night, you may be able to nullify this."[17]*

By invoking the distinctions between day and night and between Israel and the gentiles, Moshe highlights the absurdity of Korach's protest. If we were to take Korach's egalitarian argument to its logical conclusion, it would undermine the whole system of divisions and hierarchies that Hashem has clearly put into place. Surely, Moshe insinuates, Korach does not mean to suggest that we extend equal prestige and an even distribution of privilege to the gentile nations. Certainly, he concedes that a hierarchy of nations, with Israel at the pinnacle representing the ideal, is necessary for the success of humanity. Likewise, Moshe argues, a hierarchy of status within the nation of Israel is essential for its success.

This stratification, as Moshe stresses, includes Kohanim but is not limited to them. The king, judges, tribal princes, Torah scholars,

---

12   Ibid. 16:5.
13   *Bereishis* 1:5.
14   Ibid. 1:4.
15   *Vayikra* 20:26.
16   *Divrei Hayamim I* 23:13.
17   *Bamidbar Rabbah* 18:7.

parents, and teachers are also part of the extensive hierarchy that constitutes a healthy Jewish society. Because humanity has a tendency to become arrogant and neglectful of Hashem, a hierarchy of individuals or groups who are deemed more significant is humbling. Moreover, these personalities that are held in a higher regard project a nobility and grandeur that can inspire the people and serve as an ideal to strive for. Additionally, the admiration and honor that permeate society as a result will inevitably be directed beyond these positions toward Hashem, Himself.

Another status that exists in this non-egalitarian scheme is that of the master. A society organized by hierarchy in order to promote and preserve a proper attitude toward Hashem will naturally sanction a master-servant relationship. After all, the master-servant dynamic is a microcosm of our very relationship with Hashem. The vivid image of the deferential servant who lifts his eyes toward his master is indispensable in a society that must always be mindful of its Master. Although the institution of *eved Ivri* is vulnerable to abuse and can potentially threaten Hashem's rights, the benefits outweigh the risks. This is especially true when the Torah closely regulates the institution, reducing the likelihood of any abuse.

The inherent dilemmas of the *eved Ivri* institution can also be identified in the Torah hierarchical system in general. The position that egalitarianism is a better system has its merits. A society where everyone enjoys equal status is truly safer from the possibility that some individual or group will abuse their power and dehumanize those who are subordinate to them. At the same time, however, egalitarianism induces secularization, the process where G-d's presence in everyday life decreases. While the equal worth of all human beings—predicated on the idea that all have been created in the image of G-d—is a Torah value, so is humility and the awareness that we are all subservient to Hashem. Like with the relationship between freedom and security or between economic freedom and equality, regarding which it is impossible to have both completely, so too with equality and worship. Unhindered freedom, whereby there are no encroachments on privacy or restrictions on movement, sacrifices a society's security. Uninhibited capitalism, without any market regulations, creates gross economic inequality. Similarly, a society in which everyone enjoys the same status and whose citizens do not recognize that others could be more significant sacrifices the necessary cultural conditions for the proper worship of G-d.

That this is a trade-off—having a hierarchy at the cost of less equality and the potential abuse of power—is acknowledged by the Torah in its presentation of the second day of creation. After Hashem completes the creations of each and every day, He reflects and comments that his work of that day "was good."[18] Yet, after Hashem creates the firmament and divides between the upper and lower waters, He does not remark that it "was good."[19] Some commentators suggest that Hashem refrains from commending His work on the second day because His creation comes at a cost. By separating the waters, He introduces the idea of divisions and hierarchies, which breed class contention and the potential for the abuse of power.[20] Still, Hashem does create the world in this way, sanctioning divisions and hierarchies, because the costs of such a system are outweighed by its benefits: *For everything was created for His glory.*[21]

---

18   *Bereishis* 1:4, 12, 18, 21, and 31.

19   See *Rashi*, *Bereishis* 1:7, who notices this omission and for his resolution there.

20   They base this insight on the Gemara in BT *Shabbos* 156a: "One who was born on the second day of the week, will be a short-tempered person. What is the reason for this? It is because on that day, the second day of creation, the upper and lower waters were divided. Therefore, it is a day of contentiousness."

21   BT *Kesubos* 8a.

Bechukosai

Curses, Chloroform, and Marriage Contracts

IN THE 1800S, when anesthetics such as chloroform and ether were first discovered and introduced into delivery rooms, the practice was condemned by Catholics and Protestants alike. Because G-d had ordained that Eve and her descendants would suffer greatly during childbirth—"in pain you will bear children"[1]—many Christians considered any efforts to mitigate the pain of labor as blasphemous. In medieval times, before the discovery of anesthesia, any attempts, however futile, to ease the suffering of childbirth warranted the death penalty. This sanctimonious stance prevailed until 1949, when painless childbirth was finally considered acceptable by papal decree.[2]

---

1   *Bereishis* 3:1.
2   Rabbi Immanuel Jakobovitz, quoted by Dr. Avrahom Steinberg, "Natural Childbirth: May the Husband Attend?" *Halachah and Contemporary Society* (RJJ School Press, 1981), p. 54.

The attitude of Christian authorities toward the curse of Eve and its consequences for women is best captured by the words of Martin Luther, who started the Protestant Reformation:

> *This is how to comfort and encourage a woman in the pangs of childbirth, not be repeating silly old wives' tales but by speaking thus, "Dear Grete, remember that you are a woman, and that his work of God in you is pleasing to him. Trust joyfully in his will, and let him have his way with you. Work with all your might to bring forth this child. Should it mean your death, then depart happily, for you will die in the noble deed and in subservience to God. If you were not a woman, you should now wish to be one for the sake of this very work alone, that you might thus gloriously suffer and even die in the performance of God's work and will."[3]*

This out of touch, unsympathetic, and fatalistic position is in contradistinction to a Torah worldview. Rabbi Meir Simchah of Dvinsk, for example, justifies the exemption of all women from the mitzvah of procreation on the grounds that the Torah would never conceive of commanding women to subject themselves to the pain and dangers of childbirth. The Torah, "whose ways are ways of pleasantness and all her paths are peace,"[4] can only hope that women will participate on their own volition.[5] In the same vein, the imperative "to live by the mitzvos"[6]—and *not* to die as a result of fulfilling any mitzvah, implicitly conveys that "the judgments of the Torah do not bring vengeance to the world but rather bring mercy, kindness, and peace to the world."[7] Informed by the compassionate and optimistic spirit of these guiding principles, our tradition perceives the curse of Eve not as a commandment

---

3   *The Estate of Marriage* (1522).
4   *Mishlei* 3:17.
5   *Meshech Chochmah, Bereishis* 9:1.
6   *Vayikra* 18:5.
7   *Rambam, Mishneh Torah,* Laws of Shabbos 2:3.

to be suffered but as a scourge to be subdued. Consequently, no rabbinic figure has ever opposed administering anesthesia during labor.

This determination to promote our well-being is not limited to overcoming the challenges of childbirth but extends to any and all difficult circumstances. For example, there is a debate in the Gemara concerning a case whereby a father commits a dowry to the groom, only to see his daughter, the bride, die prematurely. The sages debate whether the groom or the father has the right to the dowry.[8] Almost every early commentator understands that the scope of the argument is limited to when the bride dies *before* the marriage is consummated, i.e., between the phases of *kiddushin* and *nesuin*. However, once the marriage is completed by the *chupah* ceremony, everyone agrees that the groom has a right to the dowry.[9] This interpretation is borne out by the smoothest reading of the back and forth of the Gemara, and is the legal basis that makes possible the curse alluded to in the *tochachah*, the admonition, of *Sefer Vayikra*.

The Torah warns that if we are recalcitrant and continue to behave toward Hashem casually, then "your strength will be spent in vain."[10] The simple understanding is that our agricultural ambitions will be doomed to failure. However, our sages offer an alternative interpretation:

> *"Your strength will be spent in vain"—this refers to one who married off his daughter and gave her a lot of money, but before the seven days of rejoicing are completed, his daughter dies. Thus, he buries his daughter and loses his money.[11]*

This curse is predicated on two conditions:

1. Divine intervention, i.e., Hashem causing the death of the young bride.
2. The halachah that a dowry, once the marriage is consummated, belongs to the groom, irrespective of the duration of the union.

---

8   BT *Kesubos* 47a.
9   See *Rashi, Kesubos* ibid., for example.
10   *Vayikra* 26:20.
11   *Sifri, Bechukosai* 2:5.

Because of the latter factor, the premature death of a bride (for example, during the seven days of rejoicing) is doubly tragic for the father. Not only does he lose his cherished daughter, he loses his financial investment without receiving anything in return, since the groom is no longer responsible for the welfare of his daughter. As noted above, the simplest reading of the Gemara provides the legal support for this tragic scenario.

However, when the theoretical discussion of the Gemara became a reality and an actual case of a bride who died soon after her wedding was brought before Rabbeinu Tam, the illustrious grandson of *Rashi*, he bent over backwards to reread the Gemara and recast the debate as one that relates to a bride specifically dying *after* the *nisuin*.[12] By framing the debate in this way and creating an opinion in the Gemara that cancels the father's financial obligation even after a marriage is consummated, Rabbeinu Tam was able to decide in favor of the bereft father in accordance with the halachah as presented in the Gemara. In doing so, Rabbeinu Tam rendered the full brunt of the curse obsolete, ascribing its realization to the dissenting opinion in the Gemara that is rejected by halachah. Now, because of Rabbeinu Tam's maneuvering, only if a bride dies at some later time, i.e., well after the wedding day, would the groom retain his rights to the dowry.

This is not the first time Rabbeinu Tam courageously used his innovative abilities to "finesse" a desperate situation. It is axiomatic that an adulterer and adulteress can never marry each other legally. Even if the adulteress's original marriage ends, due to divorce or being widowed, she is forever forbidden to her paramour. Yet, when a repentant apostate returned to Judaism with her gentile paramour, with whom she had previously committed adultery during her apostasy and was now ready to join her and convert to Judaism, Rabbeinu Tam permitted their union. Previously, it was assumed that the principle that forbids an adulterer and adulteress to each other applied to Jewish and non-Jewish paramours alike. Rabbeinu Tam, however, deftly created new

---

12   *Tosafos, Kesubos* ibid, *d"h Kasav.*

categories of thought to distinguish between the nature of intimacy enjoyed between two Jews from what is shared between a Jew and non-Jew. As a result, only when a married Jewish woman has extramarital relations with a Jewish man is the act considered adulterous. An extramarital affair with a non-Jew, however, is legally insignificant. By making this distinction, Rabbeinu Tam enabled this repentant Jewess to remain together with the man whom she loved, removing a potential obstacle that may have prevented her from returning to the fold.[13]

Yet, at times, Rabbeinu Tam was not even constrained by the accepted halachah, and relied on Rabbinic fiat instead of interpretive innovation.[14] Sometime after the incident of the death of the young bride highlighted above, Rabbeinu Tam took a bolder step: at a Rabbinic assembly convened by him and other leading Rabbinic authorities of France and Germany, Rabbeinu Tam successfully advocated for a decree that would insure a father's dowry up to one whole year after the wedding, a grace period well beyond the intent of the Gemara's leniency, even according to his own interpretation.

Immediately after the decree was sent to be publicly disseminated, Rabbeinu Tam recalled the horrific image of the curse found in the *tochachah*, and reflected as follows:

> *I thanked the Omnipresent that we managed to avoid the curse and render void its rebuke…We are fortunate that we have not endured that curse, and just as we avoided this curse, so shall we avoid all evil decrees, and good news shall be proclaimed to us.*[15]

Rabbeinu Tam's unwillingness to resign his community to such an ill-fate and his resolve to overcome the curse reflects the non-defeatist, positive attitude of the Jewish People.

---

13 *Tosafos*, BT *Kesubos* 3b; See also *Rambam, Mishneh Torah,* Laws of Robbery and Lost Items 1:5 and 2:2, regarding the concept of *"Takanas Hashavim"*—how the law often makes things easier for a repentant.
14 See *Tosafos, Kesubos* 47a ibid.
15 Syndod, 1160 France; Responsa *Maharam* 934, 844, 641.

Although, at the end of his life, Rabbeinu Tam rescinded his support of this enactment, his compassionate and optimistic spirit prevailed, and the decree was upheld by his students. In fact, later authorities extended its scope to protect a father's dowry up to three to five years after a wedding when unfavorable economic conditions would make such a financial loss to the father devastating.[16] We never submit to or glorify suffering. Rather, we believe that the Torah was gifted to us to enrich our lives and ennoble life itself. Indeed, it is the conviction that *all the paths of the Torah are pleasant and peaceful* that has animated our collective heart, mind, and spirit throughout the ages.

---

16   *Torah Temimah, Vayikra* ibid.

Bamidbar

Reflections on Counterfactuals

THE OMISSION IS glaring. After all the tribes (save the tribe of Levi) are counted and arranged into four distinct divisions, ready to march militarily into the Land of Canaan to conquer it, the Torah turns its attention to the separate count of the Leviim, who will not participate in the war, enjoy the spoils of victory, or receive a portion in the land.[1] The Torah begins its treatment of the tribe of Levi with its leadership: "These are the offspring of Aharon and Moshe on the day Hashem spoke with Moshe at Har Sinai."[2] It then proceeds to list both the deceased and living sons of Aharon, who have been singled out for the priesthood, followed by the designation of the rest of the tribe, who, in place of the nation's firstborns, will be sanctified to serve Hashem in

---

1   Instead, "they have been separated out to serve G-d as His ministers." *Rambam*, *Mishneh Torah*, Laws of the Sabbatical and Jubilee Years 13:12. *Rashi*, *Bamidbar* 31:4, asserts that the war against Midyan was an exception to this rule.
2   *Bamidbar* 3:1, as explained by the *Ramban*.

the *Mishkan*. The Torah concludes by counting the tribe and delegating the different tasks concerning the *Mishkan*. In the entire presentation, though, the Torah never actually lists the sons of Moshe!

Rashi, noticing this oversight, suggests that the Torah's enumeration of only the sons of Aharon—where we expected the children of Moshe to also be listed—teaches us that, "whoever teaches his friend's son Torah, Scripture views him as if he fathered him."[3] In other words, Aharon's four sons are indeed considered Moshe's offspring. The *Ramban*, instead of teasing out a moral lesson, offers an interpretation that fits with the plain-sense meaning of the text. According to the *Ramban*, the Torah does, in fact, reference the offspring of Moshe when it eventually counts the tribe of Levi by its families. "The house of Amram,"[4] which is recorded among the extensive list of Levite families, refers to none other than Moshe's family; once Aharon's family has already been mentioned initially, the only son left of the house of Amram was Moshe. Still, we can wonder, why does the Torah (almost) ignore the descendants of Moshe when it gives such prominence to the descendants of Aharon?

A poet once said, "For of all sad words of tongue or pen, [t]he saddest are these: 'It might have been!'"[5] We can suggest that the subtext of the entire section that gives distinction to the tribe of Levi is *what might have been*. Starting with the choice of Aharon over Moshe for the priesthood, to recalling the premature deaths of Nadav and Avihu and the consequent perpetuation of Aharon's legacy only through his surviving sons, and ending with the selection of the tribe of Levi over the nations' firstborns, all allude to counterfactuals—what did not actually happen, but *what might have been*.

When Hashem first appears to Moshe in the burning bush and outlines His plan for the coming redemption of B'nei Yisrael, Moshe demurs. After Moshe objects and expresses his reluctance to lead the

---

3   *Rashi, Bamidbar* 3:1.

4   *Bamidbar* 3:27.

5   John Greenleaf Whittier, *Maud Muller*.

people more than once, Hashem becomes furious with him.[6] *Rashi* lays out the harsh consequence of Moshe's recalcitrance:

> *Rabbi Yehoshua ben Karcha says: Every time the "burning of G-d's anger" is mentioned in the Torah, a lasting mark is mentioned with regard to it, but this burning anger has no lasting mark mentioned with regard to it, and we do not find any punishment coming through the burning anger. Rabbi Yosi said to him: A mark is mentioned with regard to this one too; that which is implied by the conclusion of the verse, "Is there not Aharon your brother, the Levite," who had been destined to be a Levite, not a Kohen, and I had intended that kehunah would come forth from you, Moshe. Now that you have angered Me, it will not be so. Rather, he will be a Kohen and you will be the Levite.*[7]

By presenting Moshe and Aharon together in terms of genealogy and then proceeding to only spell out by name the sons of Aharon and their special status as Kohanim, the Torah alludes to the stunning counterfactual of Moshe being granted the high priesthood and his offspring carrying on that legacy.

The message of *what might have been* does not stop there, though. The Torah also suggests that the smooth transition of Aharon's legacy was disrupted. Not only did Nadav and Avihu sin and die before their time, "they died childless,"[8] implying that had they left offspring, their offspring, not Elazar's and Isamar's, would have assumed the role of high priesthood. The theme of *what might have been* is even more pronounced when Hashem instructs Moshe to elect the tribe of Levi "in place of every firstborn."[9] The implication is painfully inescapable: initially chosen, the firstborns forfeited the privilege to minister in

---

6   *Shemos* 4:14.
7   *Rashi*, ibid.
8   *Bamidbar* 3:4.
9   Ibid. 3:12.

the *Mishkan* because of their participation in the sin of the golden calf, something the tribe of Levi was innocent of.[10]

Perhaps it is no coincidence that the idea of counterfactuals is expressed in the context of the election of those who are privileged to serve in the *Mishkan* and facilitate atonement for the people. After all, counterfactual thinking, considering alternatives and the various consequences of our choices, is at the heart of repentance. Only someone who is capable of considering how things could have been different had he chosen otherwise can feel regret. Only someone who ponders past mistakes, appreciating what might have been, will learn from his experiences and not make the same mistakes again.

Yet, upon further reflection it seems that the notion of *what might have been* has an even broader context, encompassing the entire *Sefer Bamidbar*. *Bamidbar* begins and ends with the command to "take a census of the entire assembly of B'nei Yisrael":[11]

- The first census took place in the second year after the exodus.
- The second one took place almost forty years later, right before the nation's entry into the Land of Canaan.

These two official counts of the tribes made such an impression on our sages that they would refer to *Sefer Bamidbar* as *Sefer HaPekudim*, the *Book of Numbers*.[12] It's interesting that a book that has so much drama—the rebellion of Korach, the sin of the Spies, and Moshe's hitting of the rock—is remembered more for its censuses.[13] A closer look, however, will show that when our sages renamed the book the *Book of Numbers*, they had all these episodes in mind.

The actual phrase used by Hashem to order Moshe to take the censuses literally means "lift the head." This unusual expression was chosen, according to the midrash, because of its double connotation and (implicit) moral challenge:

---

10   *Rashi* ibid.
11   *Bamidbar* 1:2, 26:2.
12   BT *Yoma* 3a; BT *Sotah* 36b.
13   See *Netziv*, introduction to his commentary on *Sefer Bamidbar*.

> *Rabbi Pinchas said in the name of Rabbi Idi: What is written at the beginning of the Book? "Lift the head." Note that "Raise high the head" or "Make great the head" is not stated, but rather "Lift the head." It is like a person who says to an executioner, "Take So-and-so's head!" Thus, here G-d gave a hint to Moshe with the deliberately ambiguous expression "Lift the head"—namely, that if B'nei Yisrael are meritorious, they will rise to greatness, as it states, "Pharaoh will lift your head and restore you to your post,"[14] and if they are not meritorious, they will all die, as it states, "Pharaoh will lift your head from you and hang you on a tree."[15]*

Taken together, the two censuses, both expressed with the phrase "lift the head" (which has two opposite connotations), allude to perhaps the greatest counterfactual in history: *What might have been* had the Jewish People not sinned by listening to the slanderous report of the Spies? *What might have been* had the first generation merited to rise to greatness?

Sefer Bamidbar, the *Book of Numbers*, only exists in the form that it does—replete with tragic narratives one after another—because everything went wrong. When the book finally concludes with the nation's preparations to enter the promised land, and the Torah records the second census with the same phrase found forty years earlier at the beginning of the book, "lift the head," portending this time not failure but success, one can't help but feel riddled with regret and filled with resolve to never again have to contemplate the saddest of all words of tongue or pen: "It might have been!"

---

14   *Bereishis* 40:13.
15   Ibid. 40:19; quote from *Bamidbar Rabbah* 1:11.

Naso

Dust and Ashes:
Responding to the Cynic

THE SCANDAL SHOCKED the nation. Likely the most prominent Protestant minister in America in the last half of the nineteenth century, Henry Ward Beecher, abolitionist and women's suffrage supporter, was sued by his student and best friend, Theodore Tilton, for having an affair with his wife, Elizabeth. His initial silence in face of the severe accusations was unnerving, arousing suspicion in the minds of many, including that of the judge, Joseph Neilson, who presided over the case, in what became known as the Adultery Trial. Though Beecher was ultimately acquitted, nine out of the twelve jurors having found him innocent, he never was able to remove the taint of the trial that blighted his otherwise illustrious career. Perhaps as a result of seeing himself as a victim of misplaced skepticism, Beecher once said, "The cynic is one who never sees a good quality in a man, and never fails to see a bad one. He is the human owl, vigilant in darkness and blind to light, mousing for vermin, and never seeing noble game." This scathing critique of cynicism sheds light on the Torah's own infamous adultery trial—the case of the *Sotah*, the wife suspected of infidelity.

Besides for its actual content, the Torah also conveys meaning in its presentation. That one passage is juxtaposed to another is significant. That a narrative is portrayed from one point of view as opposed to another is of consequence. So, when the Torah follows its discussion of priestly gifts with the section of the *Sotah*, our sages take notice. And when the Torah unexpectedly introduces the solemn matter from the innocent husband's perspective, "When a man's wife goes astray,"[1] as opposed to the wayward wife's vantage point, "When a married woman goes astray," our sages do not overlook the deviation.[2] Bothered by the Torah's curious presentation of the *Sotah* narrative, our sages comment:

> *What has been written above this topic, in the preceding passage? "A man's holies shall be [the Kohen's]."[3] The connection between the two pesukim is the following: If you withhold the gifts of the Kohen, I swear by your life that you will need to come to him to bring him the Sotah.[4]*

By juxtaposing the two passages and presenting the *Sotah* saga from the point of view of the husband, the Torah suggests that, contrary to our assumptions, it is the husband—not his wife—who is ultimately to blame for their predicament. Had he faithfully given the Kohen his dues, the husband would have avoided the need to drag his wife before the Kohen for an interrogation. Notwithstanding the superficial equivalence (avoiding a Kohen causes an encounter with a Kohen), what is the substantive connection between the two instances? How does withholding gifts from a Kohen inevitably lead to a fateful meeting with a Kohen to test one's wife's faithfulness?

---

1   *Bamidbar* 5:12.

2   See *Maharal*'s elucidation of *Rashi*'s comments in *Gur Aryeh, Bamidbar* ibid.

3   *Bamidbar* 5:10.

4   BT *Berachos* 63a, quoted by *Rashi, Bamidbar* 5:12.

When, unforgettably, Hashem commands Avraham Avinu, "*Lech lecha*—Go for yourself from your land, from your relatives, and from your father's house to a land that I will show you,"[5]Avraham unquestioningly answers the call. Yet, what is not clear at the onset is, *why* does Avraham comply? What are his motives? As scholar and bioethicist, Leon Kass, wonders:

> *Does he go because he is a god-hungry man who is moved by the awe-inspiring, commanding voice?*
>
> *Or does he go because he is a greatly ambitious man who is enticed by the promises of founding a great nation, prosperity, and great fame among all humankind?*
>
> *One cannot be sure.*[6]

While we are partial to the first interpretation, confident that our patriarch was and had always been genuinely righteous, the narrative, at this point, does not substantiate our conviction. The text is truly ambiguous. When we meet Avraham, we really don't know much about him, let alone his intentions, or even why he was chosen by Hashem in the first place.[7] Not until the *Akeidah*, posits Kass, when Avraham unequivocally demonstrates that he is willing to sacrifice all the Divine promises and blessings of the future by sacrificing his son, Yitzchak, is his sincerity proven.[8]

Still, do Avraham's motives really remain hidden up to that epic moment? Perhaps we can suggest that an earlier gesture made by Avraham already reflects his authenticity and assures his legendary response to Hashem's command to sacrifice his son.

Displeased with the moral decay of Sodom, Hashem is ready to annihilate the corrupt city. Still, Hashem won't act without including Avraham in His deliberations. The instant Avraham is apprised of the

---

5   *Bereishis* 12:1.
6   Leon Kass, *The Beginning of Wisdom: Reading Genesis* (University of Chicago Press, 2003), p. 257.
7   See *Ramban, Bereishis* 11:28, where he grapples with this phenomenon.
8   *Beginning of Wisdom* ibid.

plan, he challenges Hashem, going so far as to question the justice of the Divine decision. Even after being first refused, Avraham persists, deferentially requesting a continued audience with Hashem to plead on behalf of the wicked people of Sodom: "Behold, now, I desired to speak to my Lord although I am but dust and ash."[9] If, until now, a skeptic was suspicious of Avraham's motives, Avraham's selfless and self-effacing protest on behalf of the city of Sodom should remove all doubts about his sincerity. For this reason, our sages comment:

> As a reward for our father Avraham having said: "I am but dust and ashes," his descendants were worthy of receiving two commandments: the ashes of the parah adumah (Red Heifer), and the dust used in the ceremony of a Sotah.[10]

Avraham's altruism, which silences his own cynical critics, merits for his descendants two mitzvos that provide instruction for the cynics among them:

- The ashes of the *parah adumah*.
- The dust used in the *Sotah* ritual.

Let us consider these carefully:

- **The ashes:** It is not uncommon for members of a religious community to look askance at the privileges bestowed upon their priesthood. Instead of correctly attributing the ceremonies and offerings controlled by the priesthood to Divine command, many cynically presume them to be self-serving fabrications of the priests themselves. Of all the rites performed by the Kohanim, none disabuses the cynic of this notion more than the preparation of the ashes of the *parah adumah*. First, any Kohen involved in the *parah adumah* service, whether by slaughtering, burning, mixing, or sprinkling the ashes, becomes contaminated, so much so that even the clothing he wears becomes impure.[11] Moreover,

---

9   *Bereishis* 18:27.
10   BT *Chullin* 88b.
11   *Parah* 4:4.

a Kohen who does perform these duties, despite suffering the inconvenience of contamination, may not accept compensation for his services. Doing so invalidates the ritual.[12]

- **The dust:** For a woman who secludes herself with a man other than her husband to assume the legal status of a *Sotah*, she must have first been formally warned by her husband *not* to seclude herself with the other man. On rare occasions, the wife indeed may have committed adultery. Typically, however, Jewish women are modest and faithful. So that which would have been nothing more than a regretful indiscretion on her part is transformed by jealousy and mistrust into a salacious affair. And for this suspicious husband, nothing can convince him of her innocence except a Divine examination, [13] effectuated by a holy potion composed of sacred water, dust from the Temple courtyard, and a parchment containing the Ineffable Name of Hashem.

By placing the obligation to give priestly gifts and the *Sotah* passage side-by-side, and by emphasizing the husband's role in the narrative, the Torah reinforces its message to the cynic: not only is this couple's predicament mostly the husband's fault, it was predictable. You see, cynicism cannot be selective; it is a worldview that distorts everything one observes. If a man cannot bring himself to give priestly gifts because he suspects a Kohen of ill-gotten gain, then he will one day find himself, after needlessly accusing his wife of infidelity, with no recourse other than Divine intervention, mediated by a Kohen.

---

12   *Bechoros* 4:6.
13   See *Emes L'Yaakov, Bamidbar* 5:15.

Beha'aloscha

No Eyes for Elitism

BELIEVING THAT THEIR entry into the Land of Israel was imminent, Moshe Rabbeinu implores his father-in-law, Yisro, to accompany B'nei Yisrael into the land where he will be treated well. When Yisro balks at Moshe's proposal, Moshe persists.

However, both Moshe's impetus for wanting Yisro to join them and his counterargument to persuade him to do so is not evident to the reader. What seems to be Moshe's main talking point is the ambiguous assertion that Yisro is "the eyes of the people."[1] What does Moshe mean by this comparison? Why would it persuade Yisro to stay with B'nei Yisrael and not return instead to his birthplace and homeland?

Rashi offers three possible interpretations of this unusual phrase, shedding light both on Moshe's motivation and how he appealed to Yisro's reluctance to remain with the nation. We will demonstrate that

---

1   *Bamidbar* 10:31.

all three explanations share a common thread. Moshe's interaction with Yisro is a function of Moshe's tolerant, accommodating, and inclusive spirit. According to *Rashi*, Yisro is likened to "the eyes of the people" because:

1. Familiar with the terrain and political climate of the region, Yisro will act as a guide and will enlighten the eyes of the nation as they travel toward their final destination.
2. As a convert, who might fear being marginalized socially and legally, Moshe reassures Yisro that he "will be as dear to us as our own eyeball," which is the most protected part of the body.
3. Since Yisro saw with his own eyes all the miracles and mighty acts that were performed by Hashem on behalf of the nation, it would look bad if Yisro were to then leave for good. What would the nations of the world think?

Rabbeinu Bachya questions *Rashi*'s first interpretation. Why would B'nei Yisrael need Yisro's services? After all, they have the Clouds of Glory and the Ark of the Covenant to lead them through the desert and protect them from belligerent nations. He answers that Moshe Rabbeinu was accommodating a significant minority of the Jewish People who, because of their inferior spiritual standing, were uneasy with supernatural methods and preferred to be guided and protected by familiar means. Remarkably, despite Moshe's unparalleled greatness, he was not an elitist, someone unwilling to tolerate the less educated and worthy. Sensitive to the needs of this group, Moshe compromises and tries to enlist the help of Yisro.

Moshe's sense of brotherhood extends beyond the native Jew to include the convert as well. Aware of the sacrifices Yisro would be making by abandoning his homeland, where he is a landowner and forgoing the dignity that goes with it, Moshe makes an exception to the general rule that a convert receives no portion in the Land of Israel. Driven by the imperative "You shall love the convert,"[2] Moshe is hypersensitive to the disenfranchisement that Yisro will experience and guarantees his

---

2   *Devarim* 10:19, quoted by *Rashi* here.

father-in-law that he will be beloved by the people, and proves it by offering him a heritage in the Land of Israel.[3] For this reason, even those sages who exclude the common convert from the *bikkurim* (first-fruits) declaration agree that the descendants of Yisro do recite it, thanking Hashem for "the first fruits of the land that You have given me."[4]

Finally, Moshe's inclusive spirit reaches beyond the already initiated to include potential converts, too. Moshe pleads with Yisro not to leave them because he does not want to discourage future converts! A non-Jew with monotheistic stirrings might think to himself, "If Yisro, who had seen firsthand the wonders Hashem performed for B'nei Yisrael and was moved to attach himself to them, yet was not accepted, I stand no chance."[5] Sensitive to the anxieties of "the other" and wanting to project that the Jewish People are receptive to outsiders, Moshe begs Yisro to stay.

Although the inclusiveness that Moshe models is not embraced by all later sages, it is the attitude that prevails. "The Men of the Great Assembly said three things: Be prudent in judgment, raise many students, and make a protective fence for the Torah."[6] Rabbeinu Yonah explains that the demand to raise many students is not axiomatic, but in accordance with the opinion of Beis Hillel, as is stated in the midrash:

> *"And raise many students": The school of Shammai says: One should only teach a person who is wise, humble, of distinguished ancestry and wealthy. The school of Hillel says: One should teach every man, for there were many sinners in Israel who were attracted to the study of Torah, and their descendants were righteous, pious, and respectable people.[7]*

Unlike Shammai, who insisted on teaching Torah only to the elite, Hillel was the spiritual heir of Moshe Rabbeinu, extending toleration

---

3   *Bamidbar* 10:32, as understood by *Rashi* and *Ramban*.
4   *Ramban*; YT *Bikkurim* 4:1.
5   *Sifri* 80, cited in Menachem Kasher, *Torah Sheleimah*, vol. 38 (The Torah Sheleimah Institute, 1992), p. 118.
6   *Avos* 1:2.
7   *Avos D'Rabi Nosson* 3.

and accommodation to the less refined and respectable, inviting them to partake in the study of Torah, the heritage of every Jew. Moreover, like Moshe, Hillel's inclusiveness, too, encompassed the non-Jewish outsider. Famously, where Shammai exhibited intolerance and exclusivity, Hillel patiently and passionately embraced potential converts. While "the views of both Hillel and Shammai are the words of the Living G-d,"[8] a Heavenly Voice declared that the halachah is like Beis Hillel.

And, we may add, like Moshe Rabbeinu.

---

8   BT *Eruvin* 13b.

Shelach

Shabbos and Social Constructions

FOR SOME REASON, B'nei Yisrael could not grasp the concept of Shabbos. In the wake of the grave sin of the Spies, the Torah records: "And it was, while B'nei Yisrael were in the desert, that they found a man who was *mekoshesh eitzim* (gathering sticks) on the Shabbos day."[1] This anonymous individual was ultimately executed for his Shabbos desecration. The classic commentators were all bothered with the redundant information that the nation was "in the desert," a fact we already know. At this point in the narrative, B'nei Yisrael have been in the desert for more than a year. Because of this difficulty, *Rashi* interprets the verse based on the principle that "the Torah was not written in chronological order." He explains that the Torah states that they were "in the desert" to convey that this Shabbos violation occurred a year earlier, soon after they had arrived in the desert, and a mere two

---

1   *Bamidbar* 15:32.

weeks after receiving the mitzvah of Shabbos. The Torah disparages the people by highlighting that, although they faithfully observed the first Shabbos,[2] by the second Shabbos, not long after arriving "in the desert," this individual desecrated the sacred day.[3] Remarkably, some sages disagree with the opinion quoted by *Rashi* above and assert that B'nei Yisrael were incapable of even observing the very first Shabbos properly![4]

Either way, if the *mekoshesh* indeed desecrated the Shabbos a year earlier, why does the Torah present the incident out of order and place it at a later time? Moreover, why is the identity of the *mekoshesh* concealed?

Perhaps we can suggest that the Torah leaves the violator unnamed and gives us the impression that it happened long after the nation's entry into the desert to convey that Shabbos desecration was an ongoing problem that was ubiquitous and not limited to this particular individual or discrete event.[5] A close reading of the text possibly hints to this: "They found a man gathering wood" may imply that Moshe Rabbeinu, aware of the prevalence of Shabbos neglect, appointed watchmen to inspect the camp for possible Shabbos violations, and, sure enough, "they found" what they were looking for.[6] What is not clear, however, is why Shabbos observance was so challenging for B'nei Yisrael?

It seems that the answer lies in the same seemingly superfluous phrase "in the desert." According to Rabbeinu Bachya, the Torah accentuates that B'nei Yisrael were in the desert to allude to the halachah that a disoriented desert traveler who has lost track of time must still keep the Shabbos. From the moment he realizes that he no longer knows when Shabbos is, he is obligated to count six days and sanctify the seventh, repeating the cycle until he reaches civilization.[7] Although B'nei Yisrael

---

2   As recorded in *Shemos* 16:30, "The people rested on the seventh day."

3   *Rashi*, quoting from *Sifri* 15:32.

4   As it states in *Shemos* 16:27, "It happened on the seventh day that some of the people went out to gather [manna], and they did not find." See BT *Shabbos* 118b.

5   This is the implication of the rebuke found in *Yechezkel* 20:10–16.

6   *Sifri* 113.

7   BT *Shabbos* 69b. The dissenting opinion requires the traveler to sanctify the first day and then count six subsequent weekdays, and to repeat this cycle until he reaches civilization.

were aware of the exact day of Shabbos, the Torah stresses that they were in the desert when the *mekoshesh* warranted the death penalty for desecrating the Shabbos to underscore that anyone who finds himself in the desert and doesn't observe the Shabbos properly—even if he is unaware of the exact day of Shabbos—is viewed like the *mekoshesh*. It is not readily apparent, though, why the Torah chooses to allude to the case of the desert wanderer here and not in any of the other numerous treatments of Shabbos elsewhere in the Torah.[8]

We can propose that the Torah selects this moment to touch on the case of the desert wanderer, because the case of the desert wanderer is not some minor and immaterial detail of Shabbos observance but one that highlights what sets Shabbos apart from all other mitzvos and why it was so difficult for B'nei Yisrael to conform to it, as represented by the incident of the *mekoshesh*. Let's explain.

Unlike the day, month, and year, the week itself has no astronomical correlation:

- A day is measured by a complete revolution of the Earth on its axis (which we perceive as the rising and setting of the sun).
- A month corresponds to the moon's orbit around the Earth (which we experience as the waxing and waning of the moon).
- A year is determined by the Earth's orbit around the sun (which we discern by the changing of the seasons).

There is, however, no natural phenomenon that corresponds to the week. The rhythm of the week *only exists in the human mind*. It is a social construct, an idea that has been created, accepted, and maintained by the people in a society. In fact, it is a social construct that was introduced to the wider world by the Jewish People.

Ancient civilizations, like Egypt, Assyria, and Babylonia, did have the concept of the week, but those weekly cycles were calculated based on the position of celestial objects, either the moon or constellations. Those units of time were still dictated by nature, like the day, month, and year. Appropriately, therefore, sociologists refer to them as either

---

8   Such as *Shemos* 15:22–30, 20:8–11, 31:12–17, 35:2–3, and *Devarim* 5:12–15.

"quasi-weeks" or "lunar weeks." It is only the Jewish seven-day week, which is not based on the lunar cycle at all, that breaks this trend and is revolutionary. As Eviatar Zerubavel explains in his book, *The Seven Day Circle: the History and Meaning of the Week*:

> *A continuous seven-day cycle that runs throughout history paying no attention whatsoever to the moon and its phases is a distinctly Jewish invention. The dissociation of the seven-day week from nature has been one of the most significant contributions of Judaism to civilization…Quasi (lunar) weeks and continuous weeks actually represent two fundamentally distinct modes of temporal organization of human life, the former involving partial adaptation to nature, and the latter stressing total emancipation from it. The invention of the continuous week was therefore one of the most significant breakthroughs in human beings' attempts to break away from being prisoners of nature and create a social world of their own.*[9]

Because the seven-day Shabbos rhythm is a social construct, it is only a reality within the society that maintains it and gives it meaning. This is why halachah needs to address the desert wanderer and Shabbos observance in the first place. There is no discussion anywhere about observing other mitzvos when lost in the desert, such as *kashrus*, tefillin, or even the *chagim*. While our diet, rituals, and holidays are products of our particular culture and only have meaning to us, they are not pure social constructs. This is so because they are all tethered to the objective world. Even in the desert, having lost track of time and without a calendar, with enough information and expertise, an individual can calculate the time of day, month, and year, and, consequently, daven or commemorate any holiday at the right time. As long as ritual objects are accessible and an insistence on eating only kosher does not endanger the person, they too can be easily observed in solitude, lost in the desert.

---

9   Eviatar Zerubavel, *The Seven Day Circle: The History and Meaning of the Week* (The University of Chicago Press, 1985), pp. 9–11.

This is not the case when it comes to Shabbos. It is *impossible* to observe Shabbos once one is completely removed from the society that supports its existence. As soon as a person loses track of time and cannot rely on his social surroundings to signal what day of the week it is, he has no way of reconstructing the seven-day pattern shared by everyone else. The best he can do is to fabricate his own, personal seven-day rhythm to live by until he reconnects with civilization.

This is why the case of the desert wanderer and his relationship to Shabbos is alluded to precisely in the context of the *mekoshesh*—to reveal to the reader why Shabbos observance was so challenging for the newly emancipated nation. We were the first people in history to be asked to mark our time without any reference to the physical world. As slaves in Egypt, we might have been familiar with a quasi-week, but that was based on the natural world.[10] Never before was the rhythm of life structured around a unit of time that only existed in the minds of those who lived by it. It is no wonder, then, that B'nei Yisrael struggled to internalize the idea of Shabbos and preserve its sanctity. It is also no surprise that a few midrashim contribute the *mekoshesh's* violation to a lapse in memory; he simply forgot that it was Shabbos,[11] the seventh day of a continuous cycle that has no association with anything observable to recommend it. Perhaps this is one of the reasons Hashem supplied the nation with heavenly manna in the way that He did. The seven-day manna pattern (over the first five days one portion fell daily, on the sixth day two portions, and on the seventh day no portion) intended to help B'nei Yisrael visualize and therefore internalize the seven-day Shabbos cycle.

At this point, we can fully appreciate the significance of the way the *mekoshesh* desecrated the Shabbos. According to one opinion in the

10 Even according to the midrash (*Shemos Rabbah* 1:32) that Moshe, while still living in Pharaoh's palace, deceived the Egyptians into allowing their Jewish slaves a day of rest (which was observed on the actual Shabbos), the cycle was not maintained by the Jewish People themselves but was imposed and implemented by their masters (and overseen by Moshe!).

11 Cited in Menachem Kasher, *Torah Sheleimah*, vol. 39 (The Torah Sheleimah Institute, 1992), p. 219.

Gemara, the *mekoshesh* violated the *melachah* of *hotza'ah*, carrying in and out of the public domain.[12] Again, the redundant phrase "in the desert" alludes to this fact. Normally, the desert is not considered a public domain, because it is not usually populated. However, while B'nei Yisrael were traveling "in the desert," it was considered a public domain, making a violation of *hotza'ah* possible.[13]

The *melachah* of *hotza'ah* is classified by all the early Talmudic commentators as an "inferior *melachah*." This is so because the activity of carrying an object from a private domain to a public domain and vice versa, unlike any other prohibited *melachah*, is not creative. The transference does not transform the object in any way. The restriction is also arbitrary. Why does the Torah prohibit merely carrying an object across a threshold but permits heaving an item up a flight of stairs in one domain? Why is carrying an object from a public domain to a private domain prohibited while carrying it from one private domain to another private domain permitted? Because of its arbitrariness and lack of novelty, the act of *hotza'ah* was not automatically subsumed under the general Shabbos prohibition, "You shall not perform any creative activity (*melachah*)."[14] Instead, a separate textual source was needed to support the prohibition of *hotza'ah* and its inclusion under the broad category of *melachah*.[15]

Still, despite its objective inferiority, *hotza'ah* is legally considered a *melachah* and warrants the death penalty like any other *melachah* violation. Apparently, *hotza'ah*, like the Shabbos itself, is a pure social construct. Its significance exists only in our minds. Informed by the Torah, our society has created, accepted, and maintained that *hotza'ah* is a *melachah*. This is why the tractate of Shabbos begins with a discussion of none other than the *melachah* of *hotza'ah*, for it best captures

---

12   BT *Shabbos* 96b. Specifically, the *mekoshesh* transferred wood the distance of four *amos* in a public domain, which is a violation of a subcategory of *hotza'ah*.

13   *Ohr Hachaim*, *Bamidbar* 15:32.

14   *Shemos* 20:10.

15   BT *Shabbos* 96b. According to some early commentators, because the logic of *hotza'ah* is not apparent, not one, but two textual sources are needed to cover all the different aspects of the prohibition.

the nature of Shabbos itself. Similarly, this is why the *mekoshesh*, when he desecrates the Shabbos, does so by violating *hotza'ah*. The combined pure social constructs of Shabbos and *hotza'ah* were ideas B'nei Yisrael needed time to comprehend and cultivate. Only over time was Shabbos finally made into an unassailable reality.

What emerges from our analysis of the *mekoshesh* is one of the greatest ironies in history: Shabbos, as a pure social construct, needs us to exist. Yet, it is axiomatic that *more than the Jews have kept the Shabbos, the Shabbos has kept the Jews.*

Korach

On Bald Men
and Running after One's Hat

AFTER HIS HOMETOWN in South West London was flooded in 1908, English writer and philosopher, G. K. Chesterton, didn't react as everyone else did. Instead of dismay, he exuded optimism. The nuisance of his town being covered by water could not prevent the romantic in him from envisioning it as a picturesque "vision of Venice." Keenly aware that his unique reaction elicited shock and skepticism, Chesterton argued that most of life's inconveniences are merely matters of perspective:

> For instance, there is a current impression that it is unpleasant
> to have to run after one's hat. Why should it be unpleasant
> to the well-ordered and pious mind? Not merely because it is
> running, and running exhausts one. The same people run much
> faster in games and sports. The same people run much more

eagerly after an uninteresting little leather ball than they will after a nice silk hat.

There is an idea that it is humiliating to run after one's hat; and when people say it is humiliating, they mean that it is comic. It certainly is comic; but man is a very comic creature, and most of the things he does are comic—eating, for instance. A man running after a hat is not half so ridiculous as a man running after a wife.

Now a man could, if he felt rightly in the matter, run after his hat with the manliest ardor and the most sacred joy. He might regard himself as a jolly huntsman pursuing a wild animal, for certainly no animal could be wilder. In fact, I am inclined to believe that hat-hunting on windy days will be the sport of the upper classes in the future.

After providing other examples of how our attitude—not the events themselves—define our experiences, Chesterton finishes his essay by generalizing his theory with the following pithy phrase: "An adventure is only an inconvenience rightly considered. An inconvenience is only an adventure wrongly considered." We can suggest that Korach's downfall was a direct result of his inability to "rightly consider" his circumstances.

Our sages took seriously the names found in the Torah. Though not necessarily causative, names, they believed, reveal character and even hint at events associated with a Biblical personality. The name Korach is no different. Korach is a derivative of the word *kerei'ach*, which means bald. According to one opinion, the name conveys that Korach caused a gap—a bald spot—in the population, since so many suddenly perished as a result of his rebellion.[1] While this view understands that Korach's name captures the *consequences* of his rebellion, another approach believes that Korach's name points to the *cause* of his rebellion. As part of the initiation rite that confirmed their role in the *Mishkan* services, the

---

1   BT *Sanhedrin* 109b.

Leviim were purified by shaving their entire bodies from head to toe.[2] This shaving procedure, which rendered him bald, humiliated Korach, provoking him to retaliate against Moshe Rabbeinu, who he believed had subjected him to this degrading treatment in the first place.[3] We can wonder, however, if baldness is inherently a humiliating condition or merely the prevailing feeling among people, including Korach himself.

This very question was debated by Rabbeinu Tam and his nephew, Rabbi Yitzchak of Dampierre, who argue about the identity of the sage Rabbi Yehoshua the son of Karcha.[4] Who was Karcha?

- According to Rabbi Yitzchak, Karcha was none other than the famed Rabbi Akiva, who was bald. This information was made known to us by one of Rabbi Akiva's colleagues, Ben Azzai, who once said, "All of the sages of Israel compared to me are like the peel of a garlic, except for this bald one (*kerei'ach*)," referring to Rabbi Akiva. Appropriately then, Rabbi Akiva's son, Yehoshua, was known as the son of *Karcha*, the bald one.

- Rabbeinu Tam rejects this interpretation outright, finding it inconceivable that, despite Ben Azzai's amusing remark, people would formally refer to Rabbi Akiva as "the bald one," something that is considered disgraceful. Rabbeinu Tam proceeds to bring proof both from Tanach and the Gemara that being called "bald one" is derogatory.

In Rabbi Yitzchak's defense, we can counter that baldness is not objectively shameful; rather, it is just a fanciful notion amongst the populace that baldness is a humiliating condition. After having been singled out by Ben Azzai for his unmatched erudition with the moniker "bald one," Rabbi Akiva reevaluated his baldness. What once might have been wrongly considered as an inconvenience of nature was now rightly considered a badge of honor.

---

2   *Bamidbar* 8:6–7.

3   *Yalkut Shimoni, Korach* 750, as explained by *Pardes Yosef*.

4   *Tosafos*, BT *Bava Basra* 113a, *d"h u'matu*.

Korach, too, could have felt differently about his newfound baldness. *Rashi*, in the name of Rabbi Moshe Hadarshan, finds profound meaning in the shaving rite:

> *Since the Leviim were assigned to minister in the Mishkan as atonement for the firstborn, who had originally been assigned to the Mishkan, but forfeited it because they had committed idolatry with the golden calf, and idol-worship is called "sacrifices of the dead," and a metzora is also called "dead," Hashem required the Leviim to undergo a shaving procedure like metzoraim.*[5]

Far from humiliating, the shaving procedure was a redemptive act endured by the Leviim on behalf of the nation's firstborns. Yet, instead of rightly considering the inconvenience as ennobling, Korach wrongly considered it as debasing. Korach's impoverished attitude was not isolated to this event but extended to how he regarded his duties in the *Mishkan*. Resentful of Moshe's and Aharon's authority and prerogatives, Korach perceived his privilege of carrying the holy vessels as a demeaning "burden on his shoulder."[6] Both of these failures of perception led to his rebellion and ultimate demise.

Chesterton's *On Running After One's Hat* was a precursor to one aspect of renowned psychologist, Victor Frankl's, treatment approach called Logotherapy. Logotherapy is primarily based on the idea that man is driven to find meaning in his life. One feature of logotherapy is the notion that a person, with the right attitude, has the capacity to find meaning in any given situation, no matter how meaningless or bleak things seem to be. The following brief exchange took place between Frankl and a depressed colleague of his, an elderly widower who could not get over the loss of his beloved wife:

> *Frankl asked, "What would have happened if you had died first, and your wife would have had to survive you."*

---

5   *Rashi, Bamidbar* 8:7.

6   *Pesikta Zutresa*, based on *Bamidbar* 7:9.

"Oh," he said, "for her this would have been terrible; how she would have suffered!"

Frankl replied, "You see, such a suffering has been spared her, and it is you who have spared her this suffering—to be sure, at the price that now you have to survive and mourn her."

The man said no word, but shook Frankl's hand and calmly left his office.[7]

By reframing the man's experience, Frankl gave the widower not only comfort but something to live for. Imagine, if only Korach, after having undergone the shaving rite, would have shaken Moshe Rabbeinu's hand and calmly walked away, feeling ennobled by his new status.

---

7   Victor E. Frankl, *Man's Search for Meaning* (Beacon Press, 2006), p. 113.

Chukas

The Case of the
Missing Yad Chazakah

ONE OF THE defining terms of the Exodus is Hashem's *yad chaz-akah*—His strong hand. The metaphor is used time and time again to capture—not only vividly but succinctly—how Hashem redeemed us from slavery in Egypt:

- At the burning bush, Hashem promises Moshe that His *yad chaz-akah* will cause Pharaoh's submission.[1]
- After Moshe returns to Egypt and experiences some initial set-backs, Hashem reassures Moshe that His strong hand will force Pharaoh to free the people.[2]

---

1   *Shemos* 3:19.
2   Ibid. 6:1.

- Daily, we don tefillin on our arms to remember that Hashem took us out of Egypt with His *yad chazakah*.[3]
- Annually, the Jewish landowner expresses thanksgiving when he brings his first-fruits (*bikkurim*) to the Beis Hamikdash and recalls, in a sweeping account of Jewish history, first the hardships of slavery in Egypt, followed by the awesome way Hashem delivered us from our oppressors with a strong hand in order to bring us to the Promised Land.[4]
- When Moshe references the Exodus throughout his long lecture in *Sefer Devarim*, he consistently highlights Hashem's strong hand.[5]

Yet, when Moshe sends word to the King of Edom, asking sympathy for the once-enslaved B'nei Yisrael and permission for them to (conveniently) pass through Edom's territory, Hashem's *yad chazakah* is conspicuously absent:

> *So said your brother Israel: You are aware of all the hardship that has befallen us. Our forefathers descended to Egypt and we dwelled in Egypt many years, and the Egyptians did evil to us and to our forefathers. We cried out to Hashem and He heard our voice; He sent an emissary and took us out of Egypt.*[6]

This synopsis of our history in Egypt evokes the farmer's *bikkurim* recitation. Here, however, Moshe downplays Hashem's awe-inspiring role and makes no mention of His *yad chazakah*. Remarkably, a *"yad chazakah" does* appear in the narrative, but on the wrong side. Despite B'nei Yisrael's attempts, Edom rejects their petition and makes its position quite clear by sending out a military presence to its border: "'You shall not pass through!' Then Edom went out against him with

---

3   Ibid. 13:9.
4   *Devarim* 26:8.
5   *Devarim* 4:36, 5:15, 6:21, 7:8, 9:26.
6   *Bamidbar* 20:14–16.

a vast multitude and with a *yad chazakah* (strong hand)."[7] The contrast is striking.

Instead of reminiscing about Hashem's *yad chazakah* punishing our Egyptian enemy, we are threatened by the *yad chazakah* of our Edomite rivals. The implication is hard to miss: for omitting Hashem's *yad chazakah* in our retelling of our redemption story, we are Divinely chastised with a menacing *yad chazakah* directed at us. Why, though, does Moshe deviate from the standard script and leave out Hashem's *yad chazakah*?

In *Sefer Devarim*, where Moshe reviews not only many of the mitzvos but the nation's experiences since leaving Egypt, he recalls their encounter with Edom but with additional information that is not recorded in *Sefer Bamidbar*. Before Moshe sends his messenger to the king of Edom, he is commanded by Hashem to tell B'nei Yisrael:

> *You are passing through the boundaries of your brothers, the children of Eisav, who dwell in Seir; and they will fear you, and you shall take great care: Do not provoke them, for I shall not give you of their land.*[8]

Not only does Hashem warn B'nei Yisrael to take care not to agitate Eisav's descendants, He refers to them as their brothers. It is no wonder, then, that Moshe, when he requests permission to pass through Edom's borders, does so diplomatically, without emphasizing the way Hashem directly and demonstrably brought the Egyptian empire to its knees, which could be perceived by Edom as a subtle threat to them. Moreover, when Hashem prefaces his warning not to provoke Edom, He informs Moshe that their campaign has inspired fear in Edom. Moshe may have taken this as a cue to overcompensate and remove any reason for Edom—their brother—to be afraid of them.[9]

It seems, however, that Moshe misunderstood. Instead of dispelling any reason for Edom to be frightened, and presenting themselves as a people in need of sympathy and not as the formidable nation they

---

7   Ibid. 20:20.

8   *Devarim* 2:4–5.

9   Indeed, this is how the *Netziv*, *Bamidbar* (ibid.) and *Devarim* (ibid), understood the command.

indeed were, Hashem was expecting from Moshe something more complicated. Hashem wanted Moshe to balance, on the one hand, a sense of brotherhood and respect for the integrity of Edom's territory, while on the other hand preserving Edom's profound anxiety concerning B'nei Yisrael's power and prestige. For this reason, Hashem encourages B'nei Yisrael to purchase provisions from Edom to show off their wealth, which has been provided to them by G-d.[10] This nuanced objective certainly demands Moshe to formulate his appeal in a tactful way, but it does not preclude him from stressing Hashem's mighty role in their deliverance from centuries of persecution. On the contrary, Moshe should have *highlighted* Hashem's *yad chazakah* in order to preserve Edom's awe of B'nei Yisrael and Hashem, their G-d.

Because Moshe misinterprets, overcompensates, and omits Hashem's *yad chazakah*, B'nei Yisrael's formidability is undermined. As a result, Edom, no longer intimidated, confronts and threatens them with their *yad chazakah*.

The timeless message of the displaced *yad chazakah* is this: While we should not see ourselves as separate from the rest of humanity and should always be mindful of our common ground, we can never forget or let others forget that we are Hashem's chosen people and that He is the all-powerful Master of the world, the One Who wields a *yad chazakah*.

---

10   *Rashi, Devarim* 2:6–7.

Balak

Television Watching, Talking Pets, and Prophesying

IN LIGHT OF everyday atrocities perpetrated in the past—ones which, at the time, were deemed necessary if not virtuous, such as American slavery and lobotomies—renowned historian and biographer David McCullough was asked which contemporary socially acceptable practices he thinks future generations will look back on with disbelief. McCullough, with a mixture of sobriety and humor, responded: How is it that we watched so much television?

While McCullough highlighted mindless television watching, in general, as a widespread social malady, let us examine a particularly pernicious brand of television watching that exists only amongst the few in order to better appreciate the enigmatic story of Bilaam and his talking donkey.

Growing frustrated and not understanding why his donkey repeatedly stops on the road on his way to plot with Balak against the

Jewish People, Bilaam strikes his animal three times. Unexpectedly, in response, "Hashem opened the mouth of the she-donkey and it said to Bilaam, 'What have I done to you that you struck me these three times?'"[1] Our sages, ever sensitive to the nuances of the text, observe that the phrase "three times (*shalosh regalim*)" is the exact phrase used when the Torah commands the thrice annual pilgrimage to the Beis Hamikdash: "Three times (*shalosh regalim*) shall you celebrate for Me during the year."[2] Consequently, our sages derive that Bilaam's donkey was not just complaining but warning him of the futility of his plans, as if to say incredulously, "Are you truly seeking to undermine a nation that celebrates pilgrimage festivals three times a year!?"[3]

The interaction between Bilaam and his donkey is astounding.

- First, why does Hashem enlist the aid of an animal to chastise Bilaam, and why does He inspire it to do the unthinkable—to open its mouth and speak? Surely, there are other, more conventional ways to grab Bilaam's attention.
- Lastly, what is the connection between Bilaam and his attempt to curse the Jewish People, on the one hand, and our practice to pay homage to Hashem three times a year in the Beis Hamikdash, on the other? In what way does the latter suggest failure for the former?

In an essay on television viewing habits, American writer David Foster Wallace identifies what he calls "malignant TV-watching cycles." While many watch television for casual entertainment, there is a significant minority that do so to escape social anxiety. Individuals who cannot cope with the routine demands of human relationships, who cannot handle expectations, curtailment, and criticism, often find a substitute in television personalities. Being able to see but not be seen by the fictional characters on the screen offers companionship without the discomfort attached to real-life human relationships. In turn, a vicious cycle is triggered, as the disconnect deepens and their ability

---

1   *Bamidbar* 22:28.
2   *Shemos* 23:14.
3   Cited in *Rashi, Bamidbar* ibid.

to engage meaningfully with real people atrophies, driving them even more desperately to the comfortable confines of television watching. In his own words:

> *Concrete illustrations of malignant TV-watching cycles aren't hard to come by. If it's true that many Americans are lonely, and if it's true that many lonely people are prodigious TV-watchers, and if it's true that lonely people find in television's 2D images relief from the pain of their reluctance to be around real humans, then it's also obvious that the more time spent watching TV, the less time spent in the real human world, and the less time spent in the real human world, the harder it becomes not to feel alienated from real humans, solipsistic, lonely.*
>
> *It's also true that to the extent one begins to view pseudo-relationships with [TV fictional characters] as acceptable alternatives to relationships with real humans, one has commensurately less conscious incentive even to try to connect with real 3D persons—connections that are pretty important to mental health.*[4]

Another type of modern technology that enables us to satisfy social needs without having to be observed by others is social media applications. Recent studies have found that texting, as opposed to face-to-face communication, provides individuals with similar anxiety-reducing benefits as it minimizes the demands placed on us during in-person interactions. When texting, one has more time to respond and has no need to be concerned with the nuances of body language—both those we project and are expected to process. Overall, texting is less pressurized and less complex.[5] Likewise, the numerous Facebook "friends"

---

4   David Foster Wallace, "E Unibus Pluram: Television and U.S. Fiction," *Review of Contemporary Fiction*, 13:2 (Summer 1993), pp. 163–64.

5   Theresa E. DiDonato, "Is Constant Texting Good or Bad for Your Relationship?" *Psychology Today* (2014), www.psychologytoday.com/us/blog/meet-catch-and-keep/201403/is-constant-texting-good-or-bad-your-relationship.

that one never interacts with face-to-face create an illusory feeling of belonging without the usual demands of true friendship.

Escape from unwanted disapproving eyes is not limited to the usage of technological devices. For some, the anguish and anxiety that comes with being scrutinized by our counterparts results in establishing relationships not with fictional characters, but with animals. Unlike humans, pets love us unconditionally and do not make demands on us. The best part is that we can make all kinds of assumptions about our animals, projecting any thought or emotion onto our pets without any accountability. After all, pets cannot tell us we are wrong.

If a person reluctant to socialize was compelled to do so for, say, financial reasons, his choice profession would be one in which there would be no room for conflict, no excuse for critical feedback, no reason to compromise, where the provider would be able to tell his customer exactly what they wanted to hear. Like a dream interpreter.

One of the exegetical tools our sages use to glean information and insight is the dissection of Biblical names and places. An examination of the name, Bilaam, and his locale, Pesorah, produces three significant details:

- *B'lo Am*—He was without a people.
- *Ba al Be'iroh*—He was intimate with his donkey.[6]
- *Poter Cholomos Hayah*—He was a dream interpreter.[7]

The picture painted by our sages is clear: Bilaam was a loner, who substituted his animal for a human partner, and who, undoubtedly, deliberately pleased his patrons with positive prognostications.[8]

This biographical sketch explains the inexplicable: that Bilaam's level of prophecy reached the level of Moshe Rabbeinu. In its last passage, the Torah, after recording the death of Moshe, testifies that "never again has there arisen in Israel a prophet like Moshe, whom Hashem

---

6   According to our sages, the name "Bilaam" is a contraction of the elliptical phrase *"Ba al"* (intimate with), which omits with whom he was intimate. Based on contextual clues, our sages understood it to mean that he was intimate with *be'iroh*, his animal.

7   *Midrash Aggadah, Parashas Balak* 22. See also *Rashi, Bamidbar* 22:30.

8   As the Gemara in BT *Berachos* 55b states, "The import of a dream follows its interpretation."

had known face to face."[9] Our sages infer that *in Israel* no one has ever enjoyed the clarity attained by Moshe, but amongst the gentile nations, there has risen such a prophet—Bilaam![10] The Maharil Diskin justifies this unexpected equation as follows. First, he distinguishes between two basic categories of prophecy:

1. An ambiguous prophecy, where the prophet has input. The prophecy is designed in a way that is open, within limits, for interpretation, which invites the prophet to incorporate his unique perspective in determining the meaning of the message.[11]

2. An unambiguous prophecy, where the prophet has no input. The prophecy is designed in such a way that there is no more than one interpretation of the original message. The prophet's role is merely that of a messenger.

Except for Moshe Rabbeinu, all prophets and their prophecies fall into the first category. Since Moshe was elected and tasked to deliver the Torah, the literal and inerrant Word of Hashem, his prophecy demanded to be unambiguous, leaving no room for human input. In other words, Moshe's unparalleled greatness identified him as the prophet to receive the "ultimate prophecy" that allowed for no ambiguity.

Bilaam, on the other hand, precisely because of his moral and social shortcomings, was not trusted with any prophecy regarding the Jewish People other than an unambiguous one. As a recluse engrossed in bestiality, Bilaam lived in his own bubble, disconnected from other people, from other viewpoints, and from any external standard by which to measure his ideas, values, and behavior. He observed the world with extreme egocentrism, with an outlook limited to his concerns and needs exclusively. Consequently, Bilaam had a severely compromised sense of objectivity, unable to see reality for what it really is. This nurtured his ability to become an expert manipulator of information, capable of contorting any data to fit his agenda, making him a sought-after

---

9   *Devarim* 34:10.

10   *Sifri* ibid.

11   This, says Maharil Diskin, is the deeper meaning behind the Gemara's teaching that "each prophet prophesied in his own style."

dream interpreter. That's why he was confident he could get away with cursing the Jewish People. Any intended blessing would become fodder for him to transpose into a devastating curse. As a result, Hashem had no choice but to communicate with Bilaam on the level of prophecy of Moshe, unambiguously, with the utmost clarity, thereby straitjacketing Bilaam, rendering him a mere conduit of information.[12]

What better way to warn Bilaam of his relegated role and imminent failure than through his hitherto compliant pet? Absorbed in his own world, removed from anyone's critical or demanding gaze, Bilaam serenely sets out to fix his eyes on and curse the Jewish People. On the way, however, the protective bubble he has created for himself disintegrates when his donkey shows a mind of its own by disobediently turning off the road and then opening its mouth to rebuke him. On one level, it voices its private grievance for being mistreated by Bilaam. On another level, it warns Bilaam of his futile mission. For his target is a nation that is enjoined, "Three times a year, all your males should *be seen* before Hashem, your G-d…"[13] When the people of Israel ascend to the Beis Hamikdash three times a year to celebrate their pilgrimage festivals, they do so with the intent to not only behold the Temple's majesty but to be seen by the King—to be judged whether they have lived up to His many demands. Subjecting ourselves to this thrice-annual scrutiny conditions us to become a morally and socially robust people, able to engage productively and influentially not only with each other but with the sundry nations of the world.

Unlike Bilaam, who craves to see without being seen, the Jewish nation seeks out an external standard by which to measure itself and reality. A self-absorbed loner who lives only with his donkey in order to evade any moral and social expectations is no match for a nation that is eager to be seen thrice a year by Hashem Himself, the ultimate arbiter of the truth and of the right and of the good.

---

12   Maharil Diskin, *An Essay on the Occasion of Completing the Torah*, at the end of his commentary to the Torah, pp. 148–49. Maharil Diskin, though, doesn't discuss why Hashem chose, of all the gentiles, the fundamentally flawed Bilaam to be their representative.

13   *Devarim* 16:16.

Pinchas

The Anatomy of a Lunar Eclipse

ASTRONOMERS RECOGNIZE THREE kinds of lunar eclipses:

- The first type occurs when the moon passes, not directly behind the earth, but through an outer, faint shadow cast by the earth. The effect is quite subtle and virtually unnoticeable to an amateur.
- The second, what is known as a *partial eclipse*, occurs when the moon passes partially through the earth's inner, more distinct shadow. From earth, in mid-eclipse, one can see that a piece of the moon is darkened and obscured by the earth's shadow.
- The third type is a *total lunar eclipse*, whereby the entire moon passes directly behind the earth, through its inner shadow. The reddening of the moon during this event cannot be missed even by the most casual observer.

These three degrees of lunar obscuration have a parallel in the Jewish calendar every year when Rosh Hashanah and Rosh Chodesh overlap on the first day of the month of Tishrei.

The defining feature of Rosh Hashanah, the Day of Judgment, is the sounding of the shofar. This central obligation is first expressed in *Sefer Bamidbar*, where the Torah gives Rosh Hashanah the moniker, "A Day of Shofar Blasts,"[1] and is later reiterated in *Tehillim*, "Blow the shofar at the moon's renewal (*ba'chodesh*), at the time appointed (*ba'keseh*) for our festive day."[2] This translation of the verse in *Tehillim* follows the opinion of Rabbeinu Tam. However, Rabbeinu Meshulam dissents and translates the word *keseh* as "concealment": "Sound the shofar on our festive day (Rosh Hashanah) that conceals the holiday of the renewal of the month (Rosh Chodesh)." How so? The usual sin-offering brought monthly on every Rosh Chodesh is not offered on the first day of the month of Tishrei.

According to Rabbeinu Meshulam, the verse in *Tehillim* echoes what is suggestive in the Torah when it outlines the annual sacrifices offered on Rosh Hashanah. Every Rosh Chodesh is marked with a burnt-offering and a sin-offering.[3] Yet, when the Torah lists the additional offerings that are brought to celebrate Rosh Hashanah, it notes that these additional offerings are brought "besides the burnt offering of the new month,"[4] which implies that indeed the sin-offering of Rosh Chodesh is replaced by the special sin-offering of Rosh Hashanah.[5]

Other classic commentators notice this implication, but do not draw such dramatic conclusions. Instead, they posit that the omission of the sin-offering of the new month reflects, not any sacrificial change, but a liturgical one. On Rosh Hashanah, we should make no mention of the fact that it is also Rosh Chodesh in our daily prayers and blessings.[6]

---

1   *Bamidbar* 29:1; see also *Vayikra* 21:24.
2   *Tehillim* 81:4.
3   *Bamidbar* 29:11, 15.
4   Ibid. 29:6.
5   BT *Rosh Hashanah* 8b; see *Tosafos* ibid., *d"h She'ha'chodesh*; BT *Eruvin* 40a, *d"h Zikaron*, BT *Beitzah* 16a, *d"h Ba'keseh*.
6   *Eruvin* 3:9.

This, too, is the meaning of the verse in *Tehillim* when it states that when we sound the shofar on Rosh Hashanah, the new month will be obscured. Still, other commentators detect an even more subtle concealment of Rosh Chodesh on Rosh Hashanah. Ritually speaking, nothing is omitted from the usual Rosh Chodesh observance. Rather, the concealment alluded to in the Torah and spelled out in *Tehillim* anticipates a sociological occurrence: engrossed with the greater day of Rosh Hashanah, it will not even dawn on the minds of the Jewish People that it is Rosh Chodesh, too. All our preoccupations and preparations will be exclusively dedicated to the Day of Judgment.[7]

Like a lunar eclipse, which occurs when the sun, earth, and moon align, Rosh Chodesh, the celebration of the new moon, is eclipsed on Rosh Hashanah when they annually align. Why? The question is more compelling for those who believe that on Rosh Hashanah either the Rosh Chodesh sin-offering is omitted from the sacrificial service or that we ignore the new month in our *tefillos* in shul. Yet, even according to the position that the eclipsing of Rosh Chodesh is most subtle and merely sociological, the phenomenon is apparently significant enough to be captured in *Tehillim*.

A clue as to why Rosh Hashanah obscures Rosh Chodesh can be found in the following midrash, which expresses the idea that the moon symbolizes various aspects of the Jewish People:

> *Rabbi Levi in the name of Rabbi Yosi bar Ilai said: "It is appropriate that the bigger one count according to the bigger and the smaller one to count according to the smaller. Eisav counts according to the sun, which is bigger, and Yaakov counts according to the moon, which is smaller." Rabbi Nachman said, "this is a good sign that Eisav follows the sun [solar calendar], which is great. For just like the sun rules at day but not at night, so too, Eisav has a portion in this world but none in the World to Come. Whereas Yaakov follows the moon [lunar calendar], which is small. Just like the moon rules at night but*

---

7   Ritva, BT *Rosh Hashanah* ibid.

also at day, so too Yaakov has a portion in this world and in
the World to Come."[8]

The Jewish People's association with the moon is reflected in the fact
that the very first mitzvah given to the Jewish People as a nation, on
the eve of their emancipation from Egypt, was the mitzvah to sanctify
the new moon and order its yearly calendar according to the lunar
cycle. Unlike the rest of the nations of the world that base their year
on the solar calendar, this mitzvah would set the Jewish People apart,
orienting them to not only a different pattern of time but a completely
different belief system and lifestyle. In other words, the Jewish People's
unique relationship with the moon represents their particular identity
and destiny, which is affirmed every Rosh Chodesh.

The themes of Rosh Hashanah, however, are not specific to the Jewish
People. Although its formal observance is exclusively commemorated
by the Jewish People, the judgment that is rendered and the coronation
of Hashem as King through the sounding of the shofar have universal
implications. On this day, all peoples of the world are judged: "On Rosh
Hashanah, all human beings pass before Him like young sheep, as it is
said: 'From heaven, Hashem looks down; He sees all mankind. From
His dwelling place He gazes on all the inhabitants of the earth. He
Who fashions the hearts of them all, Who discerns all their doings.'"[9]
Likewise, all citizens of the world are expected to recognize their true
King. The liturgy on Rosh Hashanah is replete with this hope. For example, we fervently pray throughout the day: "Let everything that has
been made know that You are its Maker, let everything that has been
molded understand that You are its Molder, and let everything with a
life's breath in its nostril proclaim: Hashem, the G-d of Israel, is King,
and His Kingship rules over everything."

Unlike the holidays of Pesach, Shavuos, and Sukkos, which commemorate the Jewish People's particular historical experience, frame the
country's agricultural success in religious terms, and perpetuate a value

---

8   *Bereishis Rabbah* 6:3.
9   *Tehillim* 33:12–15; *Rosh Hashanah* 1:2.

system unique to the nation, Rosh Hashanah has a broader purview, with relevance beyond our territorial borders and cultural boundaries. Since on Rosh Hashanah universal interests are predominant, it follows that its observance should eclipse, to some degree, Rosh Chodesh, which celebrates Jewish particularity.

Rabbeinu Tam, however, avoided this conclusion entirely, insisting that *Tehillim* does not speak of concealment whatsoever on Rosh Hashanah. Recall that, according to him, the proper translation of the verse is: "Blow the shofar at the moon's renewal (*ba'chodesh*), at the time appointed (*ba'keseh*) for our festive day." In fact, Rabbeinu Tam inserted into his text of the Rosh Hashanah liturgy an explicit reference to the Rosh Chodesh sin-offering brought on Rosh Hashanah. Similarly, in his opinion, the blessing that is recited in the *tefillos* of Rosh Hashanah that concludes with a reference to "The Day of Remembrance," includes both Rosh Hashanah and Rosh Chodesh, as both are referred to in the Torah with the phrase "remembrance."[10] How are we to explain these dramatically different approaches to the treatment of Rosh Chodesh on Rosh Hashanah?

In our tradition, there are two basic schools of thought concerning the orientation of Judaism toward other nations of the world. Does the Torah embody a universal message, or is it only addressed to the Jewish People? Is Judaism only concerned with its own destiny or that of all mankind? These questions are at the heart of the debate between Rabbi Eliezer and Rabbi Yehoshua regarding when the world was created and when the Jewish People will be redeemed:

- Rabbi Eliezer says: In Tishrei the world was created; in Nissan the Jewish People were redeemed from Egypt; and in Tishrei, in the future the Jewish People will be redeemed in the final redemption with the coming of the Mashiach.
- Rabbi Yehoshua says: In Nissan, the world was created; in Nissan, the Jewish People were redeemed from Egypt; and in

---

10   *Eruvin* 40a.

Nissan, in the future the Jewish People will be redeemed in the final redemption with the coming of the Mashiach.[11]

Certainly, these sages are not arguing about facts—about when these events actually occurred or will occur. Rather, their difference of opinion hinges on how to conceptualize these events. Nissan and Tishrei are not actual dates but code words expressing whether a given event has particular or universal significance, respectively. Since both sages define the Jewish People's emancipation from enslavement in Egypt as a moment that is primarily meaningful only to the Jewish People, they agree that it took place in Nissan. They diverge, however, when it comes to "dating" the beginning and end of time:

- According to Rabbi Eliezer, the significance of the creation of the world and its ultimate redemption is not limited to the Jewish People but to all of mankind. Hence, these events take place in Tishrei.
- Rabbi Yehoshua dissents, believing that all of world history has been arranged for the sole benefit of the Jewish People. Consequently, both the creation of the world and its ultimate redemption take place in Nissan.

These two schools of thought reverberate in the debate between Rabbeinu Meshulam and Rabbeinu Tam regarding the relationship between Rosh Hashanah and Rosh Chodesh:

- Like Rabbi Eliezer, Rabbeinu Meshulam believes that the Torah's scope transcends the particularism of the Jewish nation. The Torah intends to transform all of humanity. To achieve this ambitious goal, the Jewish People are called upon to be G-d's "firstborn"[12] and "a light unto the nations."[13] Therefore, the universal themes of Rosh Hashanah, which are the objectives of creation, are fundamentally independent of the Jewish nation's

---

11   BT *Rosh Hashanah* 10b–11a.

12   *Shemos* 4:22.

13   *Yeshayahu* 49:6.

particular heritage. Not to lose sight of these universal aims, Rosh Hashanah conceals aspects of Rosh Chodesh.

- Like Rabbi Yehoshua, Rabbeinu Tam asserts that the nations of the world are the background to the Jewish People's center stage. The Torah is a blueprint not for mankind, but only for the ideal society to be created by the Jewish People alone. Even the themes of Rosh Hashanah, which are universally relevant, are only there to create a proper working framework within which the Jewish nation can thrive. In other words, the universal is truly subordinate to the particular. As a result, Rosh Chodesh can never be obscured by Rosh Hashanah.

The midrash mentioned above that compares the Jewish People to the moon extends the simile and concludes:

> *Rabbi Nachman said further: "As long as the light of the bigger one exists, the light of the smaller one isn't visible. Once the light of the bigger one fades, the light of the smaller one becomes visible. So long as the light of Eisav exists, Yaakov's light is not visible. But once Eisav's light fades, Yaakov's light becomes visible."*[14]

Whether Judaism is a universalistic or particularistic enterprise may be a matter of interpretation. One thing, however, is incontrovertible: although throughout history the Jewish nation has been periodically eclipsed, with the darkness sometimes lasting for ages, its light will shine bright yet again.

---

14   *Bereishis Rabbah* 6:3.

Matos

Vows and Voting Rights

CONTEMPORARY WESTERN SOCIETY takes it for granted that democracy is the most efficient and just political system. Adherents to this creed tend to forget what Winston Churchill said not too long ago—that "democracy is the worst form of government except for all those other forms that have been tried from time to time." Political philosopher Jason Brennan, in his book *Against Democracy*, tries to remind Western constituents of the pitfalls inherent in universal suffrage, such as how it incentivizes ignorance amongst the electorate and often subjects an educated minority to inefficient policies that are products of the whim of an uneducated majority. Since a government's function is to produce good outcomes for its people, why, asks Brennan, would we perpetuate a system that doesn't perform in an optimum way?

Instead of democracy, he promotes experimenting with epistocracy. In an epistocracy, only the educated and informed have a right to vote, or alternatively, they would get extra votes. Aside from the critique of how exactly a society would determine who is and who is not considered educated, Brennan anticipates other counterarguments, like the contention that beyond its *practical* function, democracy has an *expressive* function. Even if one were to concede that democracy as a practical political tool is wanting, still, the argument goes, democracy is indispensable because of its symbolic power, i.e., what its implementation communicates: that every individual has equal value. Brennan counters that universal voting rights is not the only available means for a society to signal that each and every citizen has equal value. One need not look further than a Torah society to discover this truth.

The Torah envisions a political society governed not by the people but by an intricate network of local, tribal, and national courts comprised of the greatest sages of each generation. All legislation is enacted by this extensive court system, whose members are appointed internally by the national Supreme Court, which also has the final say on any and every given law. Additionally, a constitutional monarch is to be established as a unifying figure who is given certain prerogatives that empower him to ensure the spiritual and moral character of the nation at home and its political prestige abroad. Yet, the Torah is founded on the doctrine that every member of society is created in the image of G-d. This idea has sweeping, fundamental consequences: the sanctity and dignity of each human being and equality for all before the law.

On the one hand, political power does not rest in the hands of the individual. On the other hand, every individual has equal value. Because of this tension, there is a risk that one of these principles will be eclipsed by the other. Specifically, there is a real danger that those with political power may ignore or deny the dignity of the common person. Consequently, we would anticipate that the Torah makes use of the expressive function of the law to convey that every citizen has equal value despite the lack of political power. Indeed, we do. An example of a law whose purpose is less about achieving practical objectives than about communicating the idea of the sanctity and dignity of each individual is the law of *nedarim*, vows.

The Torah's attitude toward *nedarim* is far from favorable. *Sefer Mishlei* refers to vows as "words of the reckless, which pierce like swords."[15] Rabbi Meir interprets the verse in *Koheles*, "It is better not to make a vow than to make one and not fulfill it,"[16] to mean that better than both unfulfilled and fulfilled vows is he who does not vow *at all*.[17] Rabbi Nosson goes so far as to compare a man who makes a vow and fulfills it to one who has illicitly built a private altar and offered a sacrifice upon it.[18] The question is obvious: if vows are frowned upon and discouraged, why does the Torah recognize them? The only reason vows are legally binding is because the Torah sanctions them. So, if vows are dangerous or superfluous because of the comprehensiveness of halachah, the Torah should have rendered any and all vows legally meaningless. Instead, the Torah affirms the right and efficacy of vows. Why?

Because the laws of *nedarim* are not intended to create *social norms*, but *social meaning*.[19] By authorizing vows, the Torah communicates that, irrespective of their expertise, erudition, and empowerment, every individual, created in the image of G-d, has equal value.

The expressive function of the law of *nedarim* signals this idea in three ways:

1. The ability to create something of significance verbally
2. The type of language that affects a vow
3. The role of a sage to annul a vow

A human being's ability to create a prohibited item by mere speech parallels Hashem's original act of Creation. Each category of creation is expressed by "G-d said, 'let there be…'"[20] With ten such utterances, Hashem brought everything into existence.[21] By articulating a vow, an individual, created in G-d's image, creates new legal categories. Though

---

15   *Mishlei* 12:18.
16   *Koheles* 5:5.
17   BT *Chullin* 2a.
18   BT *Yevamos* 109b.
19   See Cass R. Sunstein, *On the Expressive Function of Law*, University of Pennsylvania Law Review (1996), pp. 2021–53.
20   *Bereishis* 1:1–26.
21   *Avos* 5:1.

he may not have political power, man's inherent dignity empowers him in ways that must be acknowledged by the legislative establishment. Moreover, when a vow is articulated, we assess its meaning not based on the lexicon of the Torah but according to the meaning given to the words by the average man.[22] For example, if a person intends to prohibit upon himself roasted meat with the expression of "cooked meat," halachah assesses the parameters of his vow based on the common usage of the word "cooked" and not by the Torah's objective definition of the word. While it is only within the expert's purview to interpret the text of the Torah when deciding halachah, the language of the Torah does not belong to an exclusive group; it is accessible to the ordinary person who has the freedom to expand and alter its usage.

That annulment can and must be affected by a sage is described by the Mishnah as "something that floats in the air—because it is barely supported by the Written Torah."[23] One reason why Hashem chose to make the relationship between this oral halachah and the written text precarious is to reflect that, fundamentally, based on considerations of the laws of *nedarim* alone, an expert sage is not required to undermine a vow; like its creation, the power to annul a vow actually rests in the individual himself. This is apparent from the following Gemara:

> *Rabbi Yona said: This is the reason [why Shimon HaTzaddik refrained from eating guilt offerings of a nazir]: When people regret their misdeeds, they become nazirites, and when they become ritually impure and the days of their nezirus are increased, as they must become pure and then begin their terms of nezirus again, they regret having become nazirites. They will then turn out to be bringing non-sacred animals into the Temple courtyard.*[24]

Remarkably, even without appearing before a sage to seek annulment, the private pangs of regret alone undermine the nazarite vow, thus rendering the guilt offerings possibly redundant and, as a result,

---

22   BT *Nedarim* 49a.
23   *Chagigah* 1:8.
24   BT *Nedarim* 9b.

a violation of sacrificing non-obligatory guilt offerings. Apparently, the annulment is based on the rationale that every vow is implicitly conditional: a vow is only binding to the extent that the individual thought through all possible consequences and scenarios. If, however, unanticipated circumstances arise that engender regret, the vow is considered to have lacked proper commitment from its inception and, thus, is retroactively rendered null and void.[25]

Why, then, does the Torah require the involvement of a sage at all? Why is the annulment ultimately contingent on the permit of a sage if the vow has already been undermined from within? The answer is for the statement it makes. The very need for annulment reflects the inherent power that resides in an ordinary person and communicates to the leaders of the people the sanctity and dignity of the individual.[26] This is why Moshe Rabbeinu introduces the laws of *nedarim* in a way that is not found elsewhere in the Torah, directly to the nation's political leaders:

> *Moshe spoke to the heads of the Israelite tribes, saying: This is what Hashem has commanded: If a man makes a vow to Hashem…he shall not break his pledge; he must carry out all that has crossed his lips.*[27]

At the same time, the requirement that annulment must be formally submitted before a sage signals to the petitioner that, notwithstanding the sanctity and dignity of each individual and the right of equality before the law, a Torah society is hierarchical, governed by righteous experts and not the people. For this reason, annulment, unlike other legal transactions, cannot be done through agency.[28] The petitioner and the sage must meet in person, face to face, to acknowledge the role the other has in society.

---

25 *Tosafos Rid*, BT *Nedarim* 22b; *Kesef Mishnah*, commentary to *Mishneh Torah*, Laws of Vows 13:2.

26 Alternatively, the Torah demands the involvement of a sage because it does not want people to make light of vows (*Rambam, Mishneh Torah*, Laws of Oaths 6:1) or because of a concern for personal bias if one were permitted to annul his own vow (*Tosafos Rid, Nedarim* 22b).

27 *Bamidbar* 30:1–2.

28 *Rambam, Mishneh Torah*, Laws of Vows 1:4.

Masei

A Tale of Two Unities

THE OMISSION is glaring. Our sages famously note the change in pattern of how the Torah records B'nei Yisrael's early journeys through the desert. From the time they depart Egypt, the Torah consistently employs the plural form of the word "encamped." Yet, when the nation arrives at the foot of Har Sinai, the narrative unexpectedly switches to the singular form. This shift is explained in one midrash as follows: "At every location, it says, 'and they traveled…and they encamped,'[1] to signal that the people journeyed in disunity and encamped in disunity. But here at Har Sinai, they were all in accordance with one another. That is why the Torah states, 'and Israel encamped [singular form] opposite the mountain.'"[2]

While this version merely highlights the socio-political transformation that took place, according to another midrash, the unity finally achieved

---

1   *Shemos* 13:20, 16:1, 17:1, 19:2.
2   Ibid. 19:2, *Mechilta D'Rabi Yishmael, Yisro, Meseches Chodesh* 1.

by the nation was a prerequisite to receiving the Torah. As soon as Hashem redeemed the people from slavery, He desired to give them the Torah. Because there was too much infighting, though, they were unfit to be given the Torah, which is all about promoting peace. However, once the nation became unified, Hashem declared that the people, lovers of peace themselves, were now fit to receive the Torah, about which it is said, "Her ways are pleasant ways, and all her paths are peace."[3]

Since the factors of unity and peace are so essential to the Torah, it is no wonder that the narrative draws our attention to it, albeit subtly. What is perplexing, however, is that at the end of *Sefer Bamidbar*, when the Torah reviews the nation's desert journeys, all of its starts and stops, including its encampment in the Sinai Desert, there is no hint of this momentous accomplishment of unity. Unlike in *Sefer Shemos*, where the Torah abruptly breaks from the plural to the singular form to underscore the unity achieved by B'nei Yisrael, *Sefer Bamidbar* never interrupts the pattern, "and they traveled…and they encamped."[4] What is even more vexing is the narrative's neglect of another event of even greater significance. Not only does the recapitulation omit any reference to the unity attained at the foot of Har Sinai, it completely overlooks the actual giving of the Torah on Har Sinai. How can we explain these obvious exclusions?

The *Netziv*, Rabbi Naftali Tzvi Yehudah Berlin, in the introduction to his commentary on *Sefer Bamidbar*, analyzes the other name given to the book by our sages: *Sefer HaPekudim*, the *Book of Numbers*.[5] Although the book is replete with fascinating episodes, such as the Sin of the Spies and the Blessings of Bilaam, the two censuses taken in the book impressed our sages the most. The *Netziv* explains that the two counts—the first taken at the beginning of the second year after their departure from Egypt[6] and the second taken almost forty years later[7]—mark a fundamental transition that takes place in the interim.

---

3   *Mishlei* 3:17; *Yalkut Shimoni, Mishlei* 934.
4   *Bamidbar* 33:3–37.
5   See, for example, BT *Yoma* 3a and BT *Sotah* 36b.
6   *Bamidbar* 1:1.
7   Ibid. 26:2.

- Starting in Egypt and extending to most of their stay in the desert, Hashem guides B'nei Yisrael in a supernatural way (led and protected by Divine pillars of fire and clouds, nurtured by heavenly manna and a miraculously mobile spring of water).
- At the onset of the fortieth year, however, anticipating the nation's imminent entry into the Land of Israel, where they will be compelled to build their society in the manner of all nations, Hashem begins to gradually change the way He relates to them, concealing His involvement instead behind the natural order of things.

According to the *Netziv*, the second census is not redundant because it counts a different kind of population. Unlike the previous generation that merited living on a different plane of reality, the current generation will function, more or less, like the rest of the nations of the world. The name, *Sefer HaPekudim*, is thus chosen by our sages to highlight the transitional character of *Sefer Bamidbar* and the fundamental shift from the supernatural to the natural that takes place in the life of the nation as the events of the book unfold.

Another way, however, to frame the difference between the generation that left Egypt and the one that entered the Land of Israel is in terms of their respective relationship to the Torah:

- The generation that left Egypt were tasked to *receive* the Torah.
- The generation that entered the Land of Israel were enjoined to *implement* the Torah.

This essential difference accounts for the discrepancy between how the Torah initially presents B'nei Yisrael's journey in the desert in *Sefer Shemos*, which includes not only the giving of the Torah at Har Sinai but an allusion to the nation's timely unity, and the way it summarizes the journey at the end of *Sefer Bamidbar*, glossing over both the Sinaitic Revelation and the fact that the people achieved a sense of unity.

This is so because, as political thinkers have already observed, there are two kinds of unity, or to put it a different way, two kinds of peace—a negative peace and positive peace:

- Negative peace means the absence of conflict. This is achieved either because of minimal or superficial interaction between various parties or because the impetus for any conflict—i.e., diversity—is not present. Without differences, when there is only uniformity and sameness amongst peoples, there exists no cause for conflict. Moreover, in this state of peace there is no manifestation of coordination. For there to be true coordination, different elements must be organized to enable them to work together.

- Positive peace, on the other hand, means the cooperation between diverse parties. This is achieved not only despite difference but because of difference. When various groups interact together in a complementary way that results in an effective relationship, they harness the potential for conflict to produce creative energy.

We can suggest that the type of peace needed to receive the Torah differs from the type of peace needed to effectively implement the Torah:

- The type of peace that satisfies the requirement to receive the Torah is negative peace. As long as there is no strife, as long as the relationship can be described as peaceful, the people involved are compatible with the Torah's ideals and are thus fit to receive the Torah. Consequently, the generation that was redeemed from Egypt, who by the time they reached the foot of Har Sinai was able to cease its incessant quarreling, was qualified to receive the Torah. Since *Sefer Shemos* is dedicated to this generation and its task of receiving the Torah, it highlights not only the Sinaitic Revelation but alludes to the attained prerequisite negative peace by switching from the plural, "and they encamped," to the singular, "and Israel encamped."

- However, the type of peace that is required to implement the Torah is positive peace. The Torah, which is the blueprint for the ideal human society, does not envision a homogenous, monochromatic society, wherein all its citizens have the same perspective, personality, and aptitude. Instead, the Torah envisions a vibrant society comprised of a federation of twelve semi-autonomous tribes, each with its own outlook, character, and expertise, whose differences are mediated and whose diversities are amalgamated by seventy-one Supreme Court Justices, who preside over this colorful federation from their seat in the nation's capital. Since the end of *Sefer Bamidbar* is dedicated to the generation that is destined to enter the Land of Israel and its task of implementing the Torah, it not only glosses over the giving of the Torah when it retells the nation's journeys through the desert, but it neglects to even mention the peace achieved by the previous generation. This is so because, from the perspective of implementing the Torah, which demands the more rigorous positive peace, attaining negative peace is not worthy of recognition.

Until this point, we have discussed what *Sefer Bamidbar* omits. What, though, does *Sefer Bamidbar* mention when it reviews the nation's numerous stops along the way from Egypt to the Land of Israel? Springs of water and palm trees. "They journeyed from Marah and arrived in Eilim; in Eilim were twelve springs of water and seventy date palms, and they encamped there."[8] What is so significant about these springs and trees? *Rashi*, in his commentary to *Sefer Shemos*, where we originally encounter them,[9] quotes the midrash that explains:

- Twelve springs of water, corresponding to the twelve tribes, were prepared for them.
- Seventy date palms, corresponding to the seventy elders,[10] were prepared for them.[11]

To legitimize the diversity and integrity of the twelve tribes and seventy elders, Hashem created these amenities to be enjoyed for their pleasure. It is no wonder, then, that the end of *Sefer Bamidbar*, which is focused on the generation that will shortly begin to realize the principles and values of the Torah as sovereigns of their own land, pays tribute to the political mechanisms that will nurture the positive peace necessary to implement the Torah as it was meant to be, for "her ways are ways of pleasantness and all her paths are peace."

---

8   *Bamidbar* 33:9.
9   *Shemos* 15:27.
10   Moshe Rabbeinu served as the head of the Supreme Court for a total of seventy-one jurists. (Mishnah *Sanhedrin* 1:6).
11   *Mechilta* ibid.

Devarim

A Peaceful Perspective

TO FINALLY ENTER the Land of Israel, B'nei Yisrael needed to pass through Sichon's kingdom, which bordered the eastern side of the Jordan River. In *Sefer Bamidbar*, we are told that "Israel sent messengers to Sichon, king of the Emorite, saying, 'Let me pass through your land...'"[1] In *Sefer Devarim*, however, a slightly different account is presented to us by Moshe Rabbeinu: "I sent messengers from the Wilderness of Kedemos to Sichon, the king of Cheshbon, words of peace, saying, 'Let me pass through your land...'"[2] Let us consider the four differences between these two versions:

1. In *Bamidbar*, B'nei Yisrael are the ones who send the emissaries; in *Devarim*, it is Moshe who sends them.

---

1   *Bamidbar* 21:21–22.
2   *Devarim* 2:26–27.

2. In *Bamidbar*, Sichon is described as the king of the Emorites; in *Devarim*, he is the king of Cheshbon.

3. In *Bamidbar*, B'nei Yisrael are encamped "in the wilderness...at the border between Moav and the Emorite"[3]; in *Devarim*, the Torah refers to this region as the "Wilderness of Kedemos," a location not mentioned anywhere else in the Torah.

4. In *Bamidbar*, the nature of B'nei Yisrael's diplomacy is not described; in *Devarim*, Moshe's diplomatic efforts are described as "overtures of peace."

Aware of these discrepancies, the *Chizkuni* quotes a midrash that suggests that not one, but *two* letters were indeed sent to Sichon: "The one sent by Israel was for war; the one sent by Moshe was for peace."[4] In other words,[5] when the nation deliberates how to approach Sichon and his kingdom, B'nei Yisrael campaign to regard Sichon the way they would eventually consider the inhabitants of Canaan. At that later date, before B'nei Yisrael cross the Jordan River, Yehoshua, their then leader, sends letters to all the kings of Canaan giving them three choices: to leave, to surrender and become subservient to B'nei Yisrael, or to wage war.[6] Since Sichon is an Emorite king, which is one of the seven nations of Canaan, it is understandable why Israel would push for war and conquest, not peace. Yet, Moshe dissents and maintains that the nation should approach Sichon peacefully and simply request permission to pass through his land. How, though, does Moshe justify his "peace plan" when B'nei Yisrael have been commanded by Hashem to wage war with the Canaanite nations and conquer their lands?[7] Why does he insist on peace?

The answer, according to *Rashi*, rests in the obscure location, the Wilderness of Kedemos. *Kedemos* is a derivative of the word "*kedem*," which means "to come before" or "to precede." *Rashi* explains that

---

3   *Bamidbar* 21:13.

4   In his commentary to *Bamidbar* 21:21.

5   It is inconceivable that two separate and contradictory letters were actually sent.

6   *Vayikra Rabbah* 17:6.

7   *Devarim* 1:7–8, 20:10–18.

Moshe was influenced by both the Torah, which *preceded* the world, and Hashem, Who *preceded* the world:

- When Hashem appeared in order to give B'nei Yisrael the Torah, He first went and offered it to the rest of the nations.[8] Although Hashem had the foreknowledge that the nations would reject the Torah, nevertheless, "He made a gesture of peace."[9]
- Although Hashem could have wiped out Pharaoh and all of Egypt with "one lightning bolt,"[10] He chose to be "patient"[11] and sent Moshe to negotiate with Pharaoh peacefully, instead.

Informed by the precedents of peace set by Hashem and the Torah, Moshe was inclined to do the same and adopt a peaceful perspective toward Sichon. This sounds very beautiful, but is still problematic: wasn't Sichon's kingdom an Emorite (Canaanite) kingdom? Peace may be a primary Torah value, but surely it cannot override Hashem's direct commands!

Troubled by this difficulty, the *Chizkuni* explains that a majority of Sichon's land was, technically, *not* part of the Land of Canaan, which B'nei Yisrael were enjoined to conquer. Most of Sichon's land was formerly part of Moav and Ammon, which Sichon had previously captured and incorporated into his kingdom.[12] Sichon's capital city, Cheshbon, was, in fact, the very first city he had conquered during his military campaign against Moav.[13]

Perhaps we can suggest that B'nei Yisrael's and Moshe's differences were a matter of perspective:

- Eager to fulfill Hashem's command to conquer the Land of Canaan and drive out all its inhabitants, B'nei Yisrael include Sichon and his kingdom in that imperative; after all, Sichon is an Emorite, and his original kingdom was exclusively constituted

---

8   Based on *Sifri* 343, also quoted by *Rashi, Devarim* 33:2.
9   *Rashi, Devarim* 2:26.
10   *Rashi* ibid.
11   Ibid. *Rashi's* interpretation is based on *Tanchuma Hosafah* 10.
12   *Chizkuni, Devarim* 2:26.
13   *Bamidbar* 21:26, as understood by the *Ramban* there.

of Emorites and Emorite land, notwithstanding that, currently, his kingdom is primarily comprised of foreign lands and people. For this reason, B'nei Yisrael advocate to send their conditions of war to "Sichon the king of Emorite" from the "border between Moav and the Emorite."

- Moshe, on the other hand, inspired by Hashem's history of making overtures of peace, looks to reinterpret Hashem's command and its applicability to Sichon's kingdom. Since, currently, the majority of Sichon's kingdom is technically composed of Moav and Ammon land, Moshe can legitimately perceive Sichon's kingdom as being outside the scope of Hashem's command to conquer the Land of Canaan and vanquish all its Canaanite citizens. Standing in "the Wilderness of Kedemos," influenced by Hashem Who is "*Kedem*," Moshe ignores the *new* "border between Moav and the Emorite" and defines the geography, not based on current geopolitics, but as they were originally. Moshe, too, for the sake of peace, redefines Sichon's kingdom as the "kingdom of Cheshbon," because Sichon now reigns primarily over Moav lands from the seat of his capital, a former city of Moav. Moshe, therefore, advocates sending messengers to "Sichon the king of Cheshbon" bearing "words of peace."

The Torah's "ways are ways of pleasantness and all her paths are peace."[14] Consequently, it is Moshe's perspective of peace that prevails[15] and informs our tradition ever since. It was not uncommon for our sages, like Moshe Rabbeinu, to interpret the Torah's intent concerning ambiguous texts in light of the principle of "Her ways are ways of pleasantness and all her paths are peace," when applicable.[16] Furthermore, our sages even placed the value of preserving peace in a different category than other mitzvos:

---

14 *Mishlei* 3:17.

15 In both versions, the message sent to Sichon only asks for permission to pass through his land, and the accountability for the war that is waged is placed squarely on Sichon's shoulders. The subtle differences in the accounts are what hint to the "two letters" and the deliberations between B'nei Yisrael and Moshe about how to initially relate to Sichon.

16 See for example, BT *Sukkah* 32a–b and BT *Yevamos* 15a, 87b; see also *Radvaz*, Responsa 3:1051.

Great is peace because about all of the mitzvos in the Torah it is written, "If you happen upon," "If it should occur," "If you see," which implies that if the opportunity to do the mitzvah comes upon you, then you must do it, and if not, you are not bound to do it. But in the case of peace, it is written, "Seek peace, and pursue it[17]*—seek it in the place where you are, and pursue after it in another place. And this is what Israel did. Although the Holy One, Blessed be He, had said to them, "begin to take possession, and engage him in battle,"*[18] *they went in pursuit of peace.*[19]

---

17   *Tehillim* 34:16.
18   *Devarim* 2:24.
19   This is a synthesis of *Vayikra Rabbah* 9:9 and *Tanchuma, Chukas* 22.

Va'eschanan

But Ruth Cleaved to Her

AT FIRST, the two women presented a united front. Yet, after their mother-in-law, Naomi, unrelentingly insisted that they return to their parents' homes and not accompany her back to the Land of Israel, the women go their separate ways: "And Orpah kissed her mother-in-law, but Ruth cleaved to her."[1]

Our sages discerned that these choices were not isolated decisions but reflections of character. Moreover, Orpah's and Ruth's drastically different responses defined not only them but their respective descendants and cultures:

> *Rabbi Yitzchak says: The Holy One, Blessed be He, said: The children of the one who kissed (referring to the four giants descended from Orpah) will come and fall into the hand of the*

1   *Ruth* 1:14.

children of the one who cleaved (referring to David, who was
descended from Ruth).²

The reason the "ones who kiss" are subdued by the "ones who cleave"
is because the former are associated with polytheism, while the latter
are associated with monotheism.

Throughout Tanach, the gesture of kissing is characteristic of polytheistic worship:

- During a religious purge, for example, only "the knees that have
  not bowed to Baal and every mouth that has not kissed him"
  were spared.³
- Similarly, pagan priests would goad their followers, "Let the men
  who sacrifice kiss the calves!"⁴
- Iyov, too, declares that "kissing one's hand" in awe of the moon
  would be a betrayal of G-d.⁵

In contrast, the Jewish People are enjoined multiple times to cleave
to Hashem:

- "Hashem, your G-d, shall you fear, Him shall you serve, to Him
  shall you cleave, and in His Name shall you swear."⁶
- "To love Hashem, your G-d, to listen to His voice and to
  cleave to Him."⁷

What, though, is the fundamental difference between the act of kissing and the act of cleaving? Why is kissing the trademark of polytheism
while cleaving the hallmark of monotheism?

According to our tradition, the first place a concept appears in the
Torah reveals its defining feature.⁸ We first encounter the idea of
cleaving when Chavah is created and brought to Adam. After Adam

---

2   BT *Sotah* 42b.
3   *Melachim I* 19:18.
4   *Hoshea* 13:2.
5   *Iyov* 31:26–28.
6   *Devarim* 10:20.
7   Ibid. 30:20; cf. *Melachim II* 3:3. Yet, Yeravam was indeed worshipping Hashem *through*
     the calves.
8   I have come across this idea in the name of Rabbi Tzadok of Lublin.

immediately recognizes their inherent compatibility, the Torah, in an editorial comment, observes: "Therefore a man shall leave his father and his mother and cleave to his wife, and they shall become one flesh."[9]

What emerges is that cleaving is the instance of two beings merging with one another as a consequence of *leaving* something else. By definition, one cannot cleave casually. Cleaving results only when someone is willing to abandon previously held affinities and readjust one's orientation to someone else. Cleaving, therefore, is more than just the blending of two people; it is a function of character development.

In her book *Divorce Culture: Rethinking our Commitments to Marriage and Family*, sociologist Barbara Dafoe Whitehead tries to trace the ideological underpinnings of the meteoric rise (and acceptability) of divorce in Western culture. She attributes this relatively contemporary trend to a shift in fundamental values—from a balanced concern for the interests of the family and all its members to an extreme preoccupation with individual interests. While some unstable marriages are truly irreparable, Whitehead asserts that many could be redeemed if the participants were only willing to readjust and refine themselves for the sake of the marriage. This expectation is only offensive to those who define dignity as the ability to act as an individual with no restraints on the self. For everyone else, such a worldview is just plain selfish and a mark of immaturity. Whitehead quotes an early twentieth century psychologist, Ernest Groves, who anticipated that the decline of the institution of marriage would come about as a result of an unwillingness to grow up:

> *Groves saw marriage as the pathway to maturity. The habits and practice of married life led the individual away from egocentrism toward mutual regard and consideration for the happiness of others. Implicit in his view was the notion of the marital relationship to be psychologically dynamic. Far from promoting emotional stunting or stagnation, marriage led to emotional growth. In Groves's words, successful marriage led*

---

9   *Bereishis* 2:24.

to a "miracle of character reconstruction." By enlisting in the marital institution, one got the chance to grow up.

On the other hand, a rigid and immature personality was likely to resist the change and "the responsibilities and limitations associated with intimate fellowship." One expression of the immature personality was an inability to shift from courtship to a partnership view of marriage...similarly an immature spouse could get stuck in the honeymoon phase.[10]

Echoing the Torah, Groves highlights that a positive attitude toward marriage is a reflection of maturity and is successfully carried out by the "ones who cleave."

Kissing, on the other hand, is a more superficial expression. It is not predicated on character development. Although kissing can signal the existence of a deeper connection, it is not necessarily an expression of intense love or commitment. After all, kissing also functions as a casual gesture used indiscriminately and in much-less-intimate settings, such as a form of greeting or departing. The act of kissing, by its very nature, does not demand any reorientation of the self toward another. Those who are not ready for a relationship beyond courting or honeymoon phase can be described as the "ones who kiss."

Similar to marriage, the quality of commitment to the Divine can be measured in terms of cleaving and kissing:

- When Avraham Avinu is Divinely commanded to abandon and go "from your homeland, your birthplace, and your father's house," he is being beckoned to cleave to Hashem. Likewise, the Torah insists on relinquishing certain ideas, requires restraint, and most importantly, expects exclusivity. Cleaving, therefore, accurately describes our relationship with Hashem.

- On the other hand, since polytheism is predicated on the allowance of worshipping multiple gods that make no ethical demands, kissing, which does not connote exclusivity or self-sacrifice, is the perfect expression of devotion within that system.

---

10   Whitehead, pp. 40–41.

The casual relationship that is enjoyed between polytheists and their gods and its dissimilarity to monotheistic cleaving is highlighted by the Torah when it contrasts those amongst B'nei Yisrael who were enticed by the Moabite women and worshiped Ba'al-Pe'or with those who had remained loyal to Hashem: "Your eyes have seen what Hashem did with Ba'al-Pe'or, for every man that followed Ba'al-Pe'or—Hashem, your G-d, destroyed him from your midst. But you who cleave to Hashem, your G-d—you are all alive today."[11] In *Sefer Bamidbar*, where the incident occurs, the Torah records that the unfaithful who followed Ba'al-Pe'or became "attached" to it.[12] Our sages, sensitive to the subtle juxtaposition of the act of attachment to Ba'al-Pe'or with the act of cleaving to Hashem, observed:

> "Let each man kill his men who were attached [Hanitzmadim] to Ba'al-Pe'or"[13] indicates a connection that is like a bracelet [tzamid] on a woman's arm, which is worn loosely. "But you who did cleave to the Lord your G-d"[14] means they actually adhered to one another, i.e., there was a tight connection.[15]

In contrast to the profound bond of cleaving, attachment—like kissing—connotes a superficial relationship that is easily exchanged for another—whether on a whim or for self-gains.

Orpah's decision to depart from Naomi with a kiss reflects an internalization of her polytheistic culture. Conditioned to relate to her gods casually without any expectations of commitment, she is unable to meet the demands of a more meaningful relationship with her fellow man, as well. Not mature enough to give up some of her self-interests and abandon previously held beliefs, she chooses to kiss Naomi farewell rather than to cleave to her. In contrast, when Ruth questions why she deserves Boaz's graciousness, he replies:

---

11   *Devarim* 4:3–4.
12   *Bamidbar* 24:3.
13   Ibid. 24:5.
14   *Devarim* 4:4.
15   BT *Sanhedrin* 64a.

"I have been fully informed of all that you have done for your mother-in-law after the death of your husband; how you left your father and mother and the land of your birth and went to a people you had never known before. May Hashem reward your actions, and may your payment be full from Hashem, the G-d of Israel, under Whose wings you have come to seek refuge.[16]

It is hard to miss the crucial role "leaving" plays in Boaz's retelling of Ruth's act of cleaving to Naomi. Interestingly, though, Boaz begins his explanation by praising Ruth for her loyalty to Naomi. Yet, he concludes his admiration for Ruth by presuming that she has made the fateful step to convert, too. While Ruth does express to Naomi her willingness to make Naomi's G-d her G-d, it is done in the broader context of her absolute commitment to Naomi.[17] It is not at all readily apparent that Ruth is motivated to convert out of a desire to "seek refuge under the Wings of Hashem." Still, Boaz perceives Ruth's actions as a dual, parallel commitment to two seemingly different relationships. Boaz's carefully chosen words describing Ruth's sacrifice tells us as much. While his phraseology evokes the Torah's description of an ideal interpersonal relationship, specifically, a healthy marriage—"Therefore a man shall leave his father and his mother and cleave to his wife, and they shall become one flesh"—it also calls to mind the sacrifices that Avraham, the very first convert, had made, having left his "homeland, birthplace, and father's house" to follow Hashem. Why does Boaz conflate these two types of relationships? How does he know that Ruth is committed not only to Naomi but to Hashem?

Based on our discussion, we can suggest that Ruth's unwillingness to kiss Naomi farewell and her determination, instead, to abandon her upbringing and cleave to Naomi reflect a character that is already predisposed toward monotheism instead of polytheism. As Boaz sees it, Ruth's choice to leave her past and cleave to Naomi implicitly carries

---

16   *Ruth* 2:11–12.
17   Ibid. 1:16–17.

with it a rejection of any system of thought that sanctifies casual and superficial relationships, whether mortal or Divine.

It is no surprise that we discover in contemporary Western society a direct relationship between secularization and the disintegration of the marriage institution. When society is unwilling to demand restraint, value self-sacrifice, and expect exclusive commitment to a Higher Being and moral order, it implicitly encourages selfishness, enshrines extreme individualism, and sanctions casual and loose relationships of any kind.

Eikev

Heroes of Uncertainty

This phrase was coined by David Brooks,
"Heroes of Uncertainty," New York Times, May 2013.

IN HIS SEMINAL book, *Escape from Freedom*, Erich Fromm posits that there is an ambiguity, an inherent tension in the experience of freedom:

- Freedom from an authority or from a rigid socio-economic system enhances autonomy and enables individuality.
- Yet, it also *frees* the person from the institutions, social structures, and personalities that have provided a sense of security and a feeling of certainty about life, what it means, and what to expect.

For example, as a child matures, becomes more self-aware, and begins to separate from his parents, he experiences a newfound freedom from previously imposed rules, limits, and worldviews. Yet, simultaneously, this freedom engenders anxiety because he can no longer take for granted his parents' omniscience and omnipotence, and is forced, instead, to fend for himself and make his own choices in a world that is filled with doubts and dangers.

This constellation of insecurity, uncertainty, anxiety, and loneliness can be overcome adaptively by creating healthy relationships with others and embracing life and all it has to offer, including its challenges. Often, however, these negative feelings compel individuals to sacrifice their freedom in exchange for the security and certainty they desperately crave. As an example, Fromm, writing in the 1940s, highlights the psychological appeal of Fascism or other forms of totalitarianism. Despite the oppressive nature of these systems, the absolute obedience demanded, intense regimentation of society, and emphasis on the collective removes doubt and provides a strong sense of belonging.

The Torah highlights this tendency to "escape from freedom" when it anticipates the Jewish bondsman's unwillingness to go free when he is granted the opportunity. Although the Jewish bondsman consciously expresses that it is his love for his master and slave-wife that drives his decision to stay, subconsciously, it is his fear of having to make his own way in the world alone that compels him to remain enslaved. Having all of his needs met and choices made by his master for six years, the Jewish bondsman forfeits his freedom to avoid the insecurities and uncertainties that he will have to endure as an autonomous individual. The mark of slavehood that he then must bear—a hole bored through his ear—reflects his slavish mentality.[1]

Religion, too, Fromm observes, can be attractive as an escape from freedom. The overwhelming anxieties induced by living freely can drive a person to submit to a strict system of thought that exudes confidence and certainty. "The compulsive quest for certainty is not the expression of genuine faith but is rooted in the need to conquer the unbearable doubt."[2] To be sure, Fromm asserts, faith can be authentic. Still, we should not ignore the possibility that, sometimes, consciously

---

1   *Shemos* 21:2–6.

2   Erich Fromm, *Escape from Freedom*, p. 78.

expressed religious beliefs are really a guise subconsciously adopted to reconcile inner turmoil. As Fromm explains:

> *Psychologically, faith has two entirely different meanings: It can be the expression of a love of mankind and affirmation of life, or it can be a defense mechanism against a fundamental feeling of doubt, rooted in the isolation of the individual and his negative attitude toward life.*[3]

Presumably, Hashem teaches the laws of the Jewish bondsman immediately after the giving of the *Aseres Hadibros* as a cautionary tale to educate us about the ambiguity of freedom and the way underdeveloped individuals resolve the inner conflict by choosing slavery over freedom. For this reason, too, the Torah warns B'nei Yisrael not once, not twice, but three times from ever returning to Egypt to escape their freedom.[4] Still, how did Hashem ensure that the newly emancipated people did not embrace His Torah merely as an escape from freedom, i.e., as a more acceptable alternative to returning to their masters in Egypt? In other words, how did Hashem know that B'nei Yisrael's commitment to Him was an "expression of genuine faith" and not a way "to conquer unbearable doubt"?

Hashem had no choice but to test them. This is the deeper meaning behind the heavenly manna, which was provided to the nation in the desert "so that I can test them, whether they will follow My teachings or not"[5] and to "test [them] by hardships to learn what was in [their] hearts: whether [they] would keep [My] commandments or not."[6] *Rashi* understands that the test was to determine whether B'nei Yisrael would keep the commandments that regulated the manna, such as not leaving any of it over to save for the next day or going out to collect it on Shabbos. The nation's current degree of compliance was a yardstick by which to measure their obedience and to ascertain whether they were

---

3   Ibid.

4   *Mechilta, Beshalach* 2:2; *Shemos* 14:13, *Devarim* 7:16, 28:26.

5   *Shemos* 16:4.

6   *Devarim* 8:2.

ready to observe the whole set of mitzvos Hashem planned to impose on them. The *Ramban*, however, disagrees and contends that Hashem was testing the newly freed nation's ability to cope with anxiety and doubt:

> *For it was a great test that they would not have a reserve of food in their possession and would not see for themselves any plan for obtaining food in the Wilderness other than the manna, which they had never known previously and had never heard of from their forebears, and they had none of the manna to keep in their possession, which came down to them "each day's portion on its day (i.e., only one day's worth at a time)…and when the sun grew hot, it melted," and they would hunger for it intensely. And despite all this, they heeded the call to follow G-d in the Wilderness.[7]*

Although B'nei Yisrael ultimately prevailed, they did struggle with the insecurity of having to wonder where and when their next meal would come. This psychological anguish is the subtext of their constant complaints about the bland manna and their longing, instead, for the fresh fish and colorful array of vegetables that were in abundance and assured to them in Egypt:[8]

> *B'nei Yisrael said, "We have nothing except anticipating the manna"—meaning, that even the food through which we live is not in our possession so that our souls should be filled and satisfied through having it; rather, we desire it and lift our eyes toward it at all times, for it comes to us with uncertainty, so that there is nothing for us except a hoping for the manna.[9]*

Although the exodus granted them freedom from oppressive bondage, it also freed B'nei Yisrael from the security and certainty that characterized their lives under Egyptian rule. Aware of this inherent tension and strong tendency to resolve it by escaping from freedom, Hashem

---

7   Synthesis of the *Ramban's* commentary to *Shemos* 16:4 and *Devarim* 8:2–3.

8   *Bamidbar* 11:5–6.

9   *Ramban, Bamidbar* 11:6–8.

trained the fledgling nation to cope with doubt and the anxieties that accompany freedom by sustaining them with manna, an uncertain and unprecedented source of food.

The name, manna, itself testifies to this objective. When the manna first fell just outside the camp, "B'nei Yisrael said to one another, 'It is manna!'—because they didn't know what it was."[10] *Rashi* explains that manna is a Hebrew-based word that connotes food preparation; though they didn't know exactly what kind of food it was, they knew it was a portion of food. The *Rashbam*, however, asserts that manna is the Egyptian word for "what?" After recording the Egyptian word that was spoken by the people, the Torah translates for the reader: they called it manna because they didn't know *what* it was.[11] The experience of uncertainty was inherent in the manna, which was an unknown entity that inspired doubt.

After testing the mettle of the people, conditioning them to accept life's anxieties and uncertainties, Hashem was assured that their commitment to Him and His Torah was not disingenuous, simply a desperate escape from freedom, but an authentic expression of love made with equanimity, confidence, and maturity.

The drawback, however, to the "manna training program" is that it might have worked too well. As a result, B'nei Yisrael would now be prone to overconfidence as they navigate life's challenges in their newly conquered homeland, forgetting that the source of any of their achievements is Hashem. Instead, the nation will conceitedly assume that "my own power and the might of my own hand have won this wealth for me."[12] Consequently, they are reminded by Moshe before they enter the land not only how they were tested by the manna but how the heavenly manna demonstrates for all time "that man does not live on bread alone, but that man may live on anything that Hashem decrees…Remember that it is Hashem, your G-d, who gives you the power to get wealth."[13]

---

10 *Shemos* 16:15.
11 See *Rashbam, Shemos* 16:15, where he brings other examples of foreign language recorded in the text followed by its translation into Hebrew.
12 *Devarim* 8:17.
13 Ibid. 8:3, 18.

Our sages teach us that a number of things were created at twilight on the eve of Shabbos, including the mouth of the earth that swallowed Korach, the mouth of the well that provided water for B'nei Yisrael in the desert, the mouth of the donkey that spoke to Bilaam, and the manna.[14] There is an uncertainty about twilight in halachah—whether the time period should be considered day or night. Or, perhaps, it is neither, but some transitional, indeterminate time frame, which cannot be defined. Similarly, the entities that were created during twilight defy classification. Their nature is elusive and they have no parallel in our normal experiences. Like the manna, twilight itself reminds us that doubt and uncertainty are part of creation too. Hashem foresaw the psychological difficulties engendered by freedom and ensured that we would be well prepared after our redemption to engage in His world despite the insecurities, uncertainties, and loneliness that are often characteristic of it. As a result, we will never succumb to doubt, and we will never escape from the freedom He gave us, even as we endure our long, arduous, and indeterminate exile.

---

14   *Avos* 5:8; BT *Pesachim* 54a.

Re'eh

The Two Faces of Galus

OUR SAGES WONDER why we specifically construct and dwell in sukkos immediately after Yom Kippur, and offer the following insight:

> On Rosh Hashanah, the Holy One, Blessed be He, sits in judgment on every living thing. On Yom Kippur, He signs and seals His decree. Perhaps Israel has been judged to be in galus (exile). Therefore, they make a sukkah and exile themselves from their homes by dwelling there. The Holy One, Blessed be He, regards it as if they have been exiled to Babylonia.[1]

In the thought of our sages, the flimsy and faulty sukkah is a perfect metaphor for exile, where our existence is precarious.[2] However,

---

1   *Yalkut Shimoni* 653.
2   This idea is also expressed in *Sefer Hamanhig*, Laws of Sukkah 38, and *Maharil*, at the beginning of his Laws of Sukkah.

Rabbi Shlomo Gantzfried, in his commentary to the Torah, finds this interpretation of the sukkah difficult. Elsewhere, our sages make it clear that it is commendable to decorate the sukkah and to enhance the ambiance by using one's finest dinnerware. Moreover, if dwelling in the sukkah causes acute discomfort, one is exempt from the mitzvah.[3] Rain, too, undermines the fulfillment of the mitzvah and creates a universal exemption from dwelling in the sukkah.[4] If the sukkah symbolically substitutes for *galus*, the opposite would be expected: any adornments would undermine the sukkah's symbolism, and discomfort would not take away from but enhance the sukkah experience.[5]

Years before she became Israel's fourth prime minister, Golda Meir was tasked by her government, among other diplomatic duties, to encourage immigration to the newly founded country. At one Zionist Congress, held in Yerushalayim soon after the birth of the State of Israel, the president of Hadassah Women took umbrage with Meir's insistence that a Jew's only true home is Israel. Responding to Meir's call for mass and immediate immigration of all Jews from all parts of the globe, she distinguished between two categories of Jews: those living in Exile and those living in the Diaspora. She explained emphatically that, while Israel is needed as a "land of refuge" for certain Jews, "the concept of *Golah* (Exile) connotes coercion and it does not apply to us, American Jews [living in the Diaspora], and we refuse to accept it!" While we cannot condone her sentiment that she, along with American Jewry, are not in *galus* and that Israel has no religious relevance, we can recast her argument and assert that *galus* does, indeed, come in two forms: Exile and Diaspora.

In our tradition, Yaakov Avinu's personal hardships and long absences from the Land of Israel represent the experience of *galus*, in general.[6] For the same reason, of the three patriarchs, Yaakov corresponds to the Festival of Sukkos,[7] which, as we have seen, is a metaphor for

---

3   BT *Sukkah* 26a, in the name of the *Amora* Rava.

4   Mishnah *Sukkah* 2:9, BT *Sukkah* 28b.

5   *Apiryon*, pp. 112–13; Rabbi Gantzfried is also the author of *Kitzur Shulchan Aruch*.

6   For example, see *Rashi, Shemos* 32:13.

7   *Tur, Orach Chaim* 417.

galus. The Torah's account of the trials of Yaakov's life, specifically of the threat posed to him by Eisav, alludes to the dual nature of *galus*—exile and diaspora.

Returning from Charan, after having been exiled there years before to escape Eisav's wrath, Yaakov, aware that a confrontation with Eisav is inevitable, petitions Hashem, "Rescue me, please, from the hand of my brother, from the hand of Eisav, for I fear him lest he come and strike me down."[8] *Rashi* notices the redundancy of Yaakov's plea and interprets that Yaakov is lamenting the fact that his brother does not act toward him as a brother should, but the way an evil person—like Eisav—would. Rabbi Solomon Breuer, however, renders Yaakov's superfluous words differently. According to him, Yaakov perceives that Eisav presents a dual threat to him and his family:

- *From Eisav*—the physical threat
- *From my brother*—the spiritual threat

Even if Eisav doesn't assault them, Yaakov is concerned that Eisav, inspired by a sense of brotherhood, would attempt to align his clan with Yaakov's. Such an arrangement, while peaceful and preferable to hostility, carries with it the risk of assimilation—not only in terms of intermarriage but of ideas and lifestyles. Because Yaakov and his relationship with Eisav represents our experience in *galus*, the implication is inescapable: Like Eisav's two faces, which pose a physical and spiritual threat, respectively, *galus* comes in two forms, what we have termed Exile and Diaspora:

- Exile—the dimension of *galus* in which we are denied basic rights, treated like second- or third-class citizens, relegated to ghettos, suffer religious restrictions, are victims of discrimination, persecution, and, at times, genocidal attempts.
- Diaspora—the dimension of *galus* in which we are granted full citizenship, protected by a system of law and order that does not discriminate, and enjoy religious freedom predicated on the principle of the separation of church and state. Yet, precisely

---

8   *Shemos* 32:12.

because we are fully integrated into our host gentile society, we are totally exposed to foreign ideas, values, and habits that are at odds with, if not anathema to, the Torah.

Because our long experience in *galus* has predominantly been of the former kind, we are less sensitive to the dangers of the latter. So much so that, often, we do not even perceive the Diaspora experience as a kind of *galus* at all. We associate *galus* with oppression and not with freedom. We (incorrectly) assume that as long as we enjoy the right to practice our religion freely, without discrimination and with state protection from physical violence, we are guaranteed stability and success. For this reason, Jews in America have, for the most part of the last one hundred and fifty years, vehemently defended a strict separation between church and state. They vigilantly stand guard against manifestations of religion in the public sphere in order to protect the country from slipping into and becoming a "Christian America." Ever since its inception, there has always been a significant section of the American population agitating for a greater religious presence in society so that the country can be truer to its Christian (Protestant) character. Indeed, a Christian America would pose a serious threat to our liberties and invite religious persecution.

Yet, a strict stance on the separation of church and state does not only protect the courts from religious influence, it inevitably divests the culture of religion, too. Without the strong arm of the state to preserve what it deems to be ideal and virtuous, there is no way to protect society from religious and moral decay. As Rabbi Aharon Lichtenstein observes, "No society can be fully open unless it is genuinely open-ended."[9] If, in the name of religious freedom, government is not willing to take a stand on religious and moral issues and intervene to safeguard its position, then there are no limits to what society will sanction. What starts out as freedom *of* religion ends up as freedom *from* religion.[10] Those few remaining adherents to religion who find themselves uncomfortably

---

9   Rabbi Aharon Lichtenstein, *Leaves of Faith: The World of Jewish Living* (Ktav, 2004), p. 20.

10   Jonathan D. Sarna, "Church-State Dilemmas of American Jews," in *Jews and the American Public Square: Debating Religion and Republic* (Rowman & Littlefield Publishers, 2002), p. 52.

immersed in a secularized society that finds public religious expressions offensive, suppresses public talk of G-d, and condones immodesty, promiscuity, materialism, selfishness, and conceit will not be able to avoid being adversely influenced.

This inherent danger lurking in this alternative to a Christian America was not lost on all American Jews. One heated debate in the early twentieth century between the religious right and secular left, which also embroiled different political factions of American Jews, was the Gary Plan. This 1913 education program proposed to allow religious students in public school to be granted a break in the daily schedule to go off-campus during school hours for religious prayer and instruction. This proposal, of course, scared many Jews who saw it as a precursor to an inexorable push toward a Christian America. Still, a leading Jewish proponent of the strict separation of church and state perceived the tension that a sensitive and thinking Jew cannot easily resolve:

> *In America, we have a unique and, therefore, very delicate problem. We, of course, want to keep religion, Bible reading, hymn singing out of the public schools. At the same time, we know that there is not enough efficient moral and religious education in the country...Jews make a mistake in thinking only of themselves and assuming always a negative and critical attitude. They must supplement that negative attitude with a constructive policy. Otherwise, they will soon be classed in the minds of the Christian men and women in this country with the free-thinkers and with those who have no interest in the religious education of the youth. That, of course, is undesirable.*[11]

While this American Jew's primary concern is any immediate political fallout from siding with the anti-religious parties in a still religiously dominant America, he tacitly recognizes that secularization of society carries with it a whole different set of threats to Judaism, such as broad social decay that will infect and disrupt Jewish life in the long run.

---

11   Quoted in Sarna, p. 61, and John Meacham, *American Gospel: G-d, the Founding Fathers, and the Making of a Nation* (Random House, 2006), p. 149.

Because of this deep flaw in this organization of society, some Americans Jews have supported a different alternative to a Christian America: a non-denominational, religious society that privileges all religions alike and which promotes and protects religious morals, virtues, and ideals. This movement was particularly popular in the early nineteenth century, but lost its appeal in the latter half of the century after it had witnessed a religious revival that attempted to remake or restore the nation as an exclusively Christian America.[12] Although this alternative version, which does not separate church and state completely and promotes a religious character for the country, is not foolproof and without risks, the need for its formulation highlights our ongoing dilemma:

> *In their dreams, most Jews long for an America where they and their neighbors can live as equals, safe from the fire and brimstone of the Christian state and the desolate barrenness of the secular one. How best to achieve such a society, however, remains an unsolved puzzle.*[13]

This perpetual tension is a function of *galus*. Either we live in *exile* and are physically unsafe or we live in the *diaspora*, physically secure but spiritually at risk. For this reason, the sukkah, which is a metaphor for *galus*, has a dual character:

- On the one hand, it is precarious, questionable as a shelter from physical harm.
- On the other hand, it should accommodate a pleasant physical experience.

The former aspect symbolizes the *exile* dimension of *galus*. The latter aspect symbolizes the *diaspora* dimension of *galus*. The sukkah is a constant reminder that, as hard as we try, we cannot escape the hand of Eisav, the hand of our brother. Ultimately, the only reprieve and answer to the puzzle is *geulah*, redemption.

---

12   Sarna.
13   Sarna, p. 64.

Shoftim

Torah, Totalitarianism, and Tolerance

AFTER ESTABLISHING THE importance of having a functioning network of courts throughout the country—in every tribal territory and in every major city[1]—the Torah makes clear that this network is hierarchical, with the ultimate authority residing in the national Supreme Court (*Sanhedrin Hagadol*), located on the Temple Mount.[2] Should a jurist flagrantly defy a decision of the Supreme Court, he is put to death.[3] The execution of the *Zaken Mamrei*, the rebellious elder, serves as a deterrent and reminder of the absolute authority of the Supreme Court.[4]

---

1   *Devarim* 16:18.
2   Ibid. 17:8–11.
3   Ibid. 17:12.
4   Ibid. 17:13, see also the *Seforno*'s commentary.

Clearly, brazen disobedience is not taken lightly by the Torah, and this is not the only instance rebelliousness warrants such a severe response. Both the wayward wife (*Sotah*) and the wayward son (*Ben Sorer U'Moreh*) are treated harshly, as well—the latter with the death penalty at the hands of a human court,[5] the former by Divine intervention.[6] Yet, according to most of our sages, there is a crucial difference between the rebellious elder, on the one hand, and the rebellious wife or son, on the other:

> *Rabbi Yoshiya says: Ze'eira, who was one of the men of Yerushalayim, told me three matters: A husband who retracted his warning, his warning is retracted; and in the case of a rebellious elder whom the court wishes to pardon, the court may pardon him; and in the case of a wayward and rebellious son, whose father and mother wish to pardon him for his sins, they may pardon him. And when I came to my colleagues in the south and told them these rulings, they agreed with me with regard to two of them, but with regard to pardoning a rebellious elder, they did not agree with me. They held that a rebellious elder cannot be pardoned, in order that discord not proliferate among the Jewish People.*[7]

Notwithstanding the potentially hazardous socio-religious consequences of rebelliousness, the first opinion allows for forgiveness in all three instances. Unlike other treasonous or depraved acts, what sets these three cases apart is their shared common denominator—doubt:

- While the wayward son's conduct is deeply disturbing, the death penalty serves as a preventive measure against presumed future heinous crimes. Projection, though, should never be confused with certitude. As a result, the system allows for parental pardon if their unique insight sheds doubt on the process.

---

5   Ibid. 21:18–21.

6   *Bamidbar* 5:11–31.

7   BT *Sotah* 25a.

- Similarly, the wayward wife has not been caught in the act, but is only suspected of adultery. Her cavalier attitude toward her husband's jealous protestations has compromised her presumed fidelity, leading us to strongly consider that she had been unfaithful while secluded with another man. Still, if her husband ultimately trusts her and is willing to pardon her disobedience, we rely on his judgment.

- Likewise, the rebellious elder does not question any explicit, undeniable teaching of the Torah; instead, his campaign challenges an interpretation of the Torah's intent. Written with an abundance of potential meaning, the Torah is—within limits—an open text that invites multiple interpretations. While the Supreme Court's rendering is decisive, fundamentally, its ruling is interpretive in nature, not objective. Because the rebellious elder's dissenting interpretation might be equally legitimate, a court justifiably might hesitate to execute him for his recalcitrance.

The majority opinion, however, distinguishes between the three cases. While a husband can pardon his wife, ascribing her loose behavior to poor judgment, and parents can excuse their son, attributing his delinquency to immaturity, the Supreme Court cannot pardon the rebellious elder who defies their authority. To be sure, when it comes to elucidating the Torah, it is precisely the multiplicity of interpretations embedded in the Torah that fosters debate, protects against dogmatic thinking, and is responsible for the fluidity of the Torah, ensuring its relevance at all times and in all places.[8] However, the ambiguity present in these three instances of rebellion, while significant, is not decisive. Rather, the primary consideration is the public or private nature of each case.

---

8   See *Rashi*, BT *Kesubos* 57a: "About such issues one can declare that both represent the view of the living G-d. On some occasions, one perspective will prove more authentic, and under other circumstances the other view will appear to be more compelling. The effectiveness of particular rationales shifts as conditions of their application changes even if only subtly." See also *Rambam, Mishneh Torah*, Laws of Rebellious Ones 2:1.

John Locke, in his *Letter Concerning Toleration*, argued for religious tolerance on the theological grounds that coerced religious gestures are inherently meaningless. Yet, even he conceded that for political purposes, religious coercion is justified.[9] This is so because a sovereign is not primarily interested with any particular citizens' wellbeing, spiritual or otherwise, but with the health of his society as a whole. Consequently, a sovereign that deems certain religious practices and beliefs as civil matters will only consider whether his subjects' public habits preserve or undermine the character of his nation; he has no interest in private convictions.

Because the Torah perceives all human experiences as within its sphere of concern, it regulates all aspects of our lives. Because Hashem, our Sovereign, considers all human matters—including ritual, moral, and philosophical issues—as civil matters, a public expression of dissent or deviance in any of these areas is intolerable.[10] All the more so, if a respected scholar openly challenges the highest authority in the land. Once the national Supreme Court renders its opinion, its decision, as far as its contemporaries are concerned, is final. As much as healthy, civil discourse is encouraged, ongoing deliberation with no end is impractical, divisive, and destructive. According to this approach, there is no room for tolerance when the integrity of society is at stake.

On the other hand, family life, whether it be the loyalty between spouses or the art of parenting, is foremost a personal matter, not a political one. To be sure, one's family culture can impact society, but that is only in the aggregate, indirectly, and over time. Unlike a sovereign, a parent or sibling *should* care about the subjective life of their loved one, about his or her personal struggles with aspects of the religion, and tolerate some experimentation and individuation. Consequently, concerning family life, the Torah accommodates experimentation and even some risk taking. Moreover, the Torah, which respects the dignity

---

9   For example, his allowance for religious tolerance does not extend to Catholics.

10   For more on how the overlap of religious and civil matters affects the scope of religious tolerance, see Eric Nelson, *The Hebrew Republic: Jewish Sources and the Transformation of European Political Thought* (Harvard University Press, 2010), pp. 88–137.

of each individual, seeks to accommodate an individual's autonomy as much as possible.[11] In order to dignify the individual, therefore, the Torah tolerates trial and error in one's private life.[12]

It is incontrovertible that the Torah regulates our actions, thoughts, and even emotions.[13] It forbids blasphemy, punishes heretics, and co-erces religious participation.[14] It dictates whom we can marry, what we are permitted to eat, and what we can and cannot do with our money. The Torah also commands us to set up an extensive court system and police force to ensure compliance. The unrestrained response to the rebellious elder highlights this totalitarian position. Yet, the Torah tempers this totalitarian stance with a spirit of tolerance. In order to preserve the value of family and individual dignity—both hallmarks of Judaism—the Torah tolerates behavior it does not approve of and gives wide discretion to the husband of the wayward wife and the parents of the wayward son. According to the Torah, the boundary between the public and the private, between the political and the personal, serves to balance necessary intolerance and healthy tolerance.

---

11   For a discussion of the justification of tolerance based on the "respect of persons," as well as a critique of Locke's arguments, see Susan Mendes, *Justifying Tolerance: Conceptual and Historical Perspectives* (Cambridge University Press, 1988).

12   Likewise, the Torah disqualifies family members from testifying against one another: "Fathers shall not be put to death because of their sons nor shall sons be put to death because of their fathers (*Devarim* 24:16, as understood by our sages, BT *Sanhedrin* 27b)." Empowering close relatives to testify and condemn a loved one would not only undermine the centrality of the family in Judaism but would also conflate private and public life and leave no room for personal autonomy. However, if an individual abuses this leeway and leverages the protective walls of his home to corrupt family members and incite them to worship foreign gods, he is treated mercilessly and is summarily executed (*Devarim* 13:7).

13   For example, the prohibition against coveting; *Shemos* 20:14.

14   See BT *Kesubos* 86a–b, *Bava Basra* 8b, *Chullin* 110b.

Ki Seitzei

A Cave, a Field,
and a Bride's Dilemma

AFTER BEGINNING WORLD War II with 176 capable destroyers, by
the spring of 1940, the British naval fleet was down to sixty-eight fit
for warfare. Desperate, Prime Minister Winston Churchill appealed
to American president, Franklin D. Roosevelt, for fifty war-ready destroyers, arguing that the British could not succeed in the "Battle of the
Atlantic" against Germany and Italy without them. And if Britain failed
and fell, nothing, insisted Churchill, would stand in the way between
the German war machine and the east coast of the United States. Thus
began the summer-long negotiations of what became known as the
Destroyers for Bases Agreement (a precursor to the Lend-Lease Act).
In exchange for the desperately sought-after destroyers, the United
States received land rights to British military bases in the Caribbean
and Western Atlantic.

By tying the destroyers to bases, Roosevelt, ever conscious of public sentiment, and especially so in a reelection year, ensured that the transfer of destroyers would not be perceived as an interventionist gesture but as a shrewd strategic move to shore up American defenses. Roosevelt aimed to present the deal to the isolationist American public as a hard-fought and deftly negotiated business deal, one in which the United States came out on top. In contrast, Churchill wanted the transaction to be viewed as an exchange of gifts between friends and, hopefully, future allies. In the end, both parties succeeded: Churchill got his destroyers and the promise of a much-needed partnership; Roosevelt enhanced his popularity at home while fulfilling international responsibilities abroad.

Although it took place under vastly different circumstances, the tense negotiations between Avraham Avinu and Ephron the Hittite end in a similar way.

After Sarah Imeinu dies, Avraham approaches the Hittite people and asks to buy an "estate for a burial site,"[1] within which to inter his beloved wife. Despite their gestures of deference, the Hittites demur and, instead, offer Avraham access to any one of their burial plots to lay his wife to rest. Unsatisfied, Avraham requests an audience with a man named Ephron, and offers to purchase from him the Cave of Machpelah that is on the edge of his field. In the presence of the Hittite people, Ephron changes the terms of the negotiations and offers to gift Avraham not only the cave but the entire field. As soon as Avraham hears this proposition, he makes it clear that he is eager to buy the entire field. Ephron quickly acquiesces and sets the price—four hundred silver shekels. Avraham accepts and, in the presence of the Hittite people, purchases the field and all that is within it, including the coveted cave.

The classic commentators address Ephron's unsolicited inclusion of the entire field in the negotiations. Some propose that Ephron is concerned for Avraham's interest: It is inconvenient for anyone and inappropriate for a man of Avraham's stature to own a piece of land

---

1   *Bereishis* 23:4.

whose only access is through another's land. Others posit that Ephron is motivated for selfish interests: he exploits Avraham's desperate situation. Contemporary scholars, on the other hand, highlight parallels between ancient Hittite law about selling parts of a field and Avraham's negotiations with Ephron. An unexpected comment by our sages in the Gemara, however, which links these negotiations to Jewish marital law, invites us to search for a more meaningful interpretation.

That a woman can be betrothed through intimacy is explicit in the Torah: "When a man takes a wife and is intimate with her."[2] But how do we know a woman can be betrothed with money?

From Avraham. When Avraham displays his readiness to purchase not only the cave but the entire field, he urgently says to Ephron, "I am giving the money for the field; take [it] from me."[3] According to our sages, since the expression "take [it]" used by Avraham refers to money, the same expression, "takes," found in the context of betrothal, connotes a transference of money as well.[4] This curious link intimates that the negotiations between Avraham and Ephron—and the role of the field—should enhance our understanding of *kesef kiddushin*, money as a method for betrothal. How so? By looking more closely at Avraham's negotiations with Ephron and the Hittites, a better understanding of a bride's interests when entering into a marital relationship will emerge.

When Avraham approaches the Hittite people with his request, he introduces himself as "an alien resident."[5] This description is internally inconsistent: an alien is a foreigner; a resident is an established local. Because of this difficulty, *Rashi* explains that Avraham means to convey that, although he was originally an alien from another land, he has since come to settle in Canaan. Precisely for this reason, Avraham seeks an "estate for a burial site." No longer interested in returning to his land of origin and to any ancestral plot he may have owned there, Avraham wants to permanently establish himself in his current

---

2   *Devarim* 24:1.
3   *Bereishis* 23:13.
4   BT *Kiddushin* 4b.
5   *Bereishis* 23:4.

location. Purchasing an estate to be used for a family burial site would secure his and his family's permanence in Canaan.

This ambition, however, is the source of the tension between himself and the Hittite people. The Hittites are reluctant to hand over any land to Avraham, because they, too, are keenly aware of the socio-political implications of Avraham becoming a landowner in their midst. At the same time, Avraham is a prestigious and powerful figure; it is not mere flattery when they refer to him as an "elect of G-d."[6] By the time of their encounter, Avraham has already bested the major superpowers of his time: Pharaoh and the four kings from Mesopotamia. The Hittites, therefore, are in a bind:

- On the one hand, they are not interested in granting Avraham a foothold in their land, which inevitably will lead to further expansion by him, his family, and his tribe.
- On the other hand, how can they outright refuse a request by someone with so much clout?

Once Avraham identifies a specific piece of land, this dilemma is shifted onto its owner, Ephron. But Ephron's dilemma is much more formidable. Not only does he have to find a way to deal with Avraham, he has to worry about the reaction of the Hittite people to whatever decision he will make. If Ephron denies Avraham his request, he will have to deal with the consequences of rejecting an "elect of G-d." If he satisfies Avraham's needs, he will have to face the possible wrath of his fellow people for undermining their national security and territorial integrity.

Faced with what seems like an impossible situation, Ephron ingeniously negotiates his way through the dilemma. His solution: sell Avraham not only the cave but his entire field. By tying the sale of the cave to the sale of the entire field for a huge sum of money, Ephron reframes the transaction as a shrewd business deal. To be sure, with the purchase of an estate to bury his dead, Avraham becomes a permanent resident in Canaan. But instead of the sale being perceived as

---

6   Ibid. 23:6.

a concession to Avraham and a resignation to the inevitable, Ephron emerges as a brilliant negotiator who took advantage of Avraham's predicament and accepted an offer he couldn't refuse.

Avraham, for his part, immediately recognizes the valuable role the field plays in their negotiations and eagerly seeks to seal the deal: "I am giving the money for the field; take [it] from me, and I will bury my dead there." The money for the field, therefore, becomes the mechanism by which Ephron saves face in front of his people.

In light of the above analysis, we can suggest that this is why our sages derive *kesef kiddushin* from the money Avraham offers Ephron for his field. A Jewish bride is faced with a dilemma, as illustrated in the following Chassidic legend:

> *As her wedding day approaches, a bride seeks her rabbi's advice. "Rabbi," she says, "my whole life I have been taught to be chaste. I have conducted myself with the utmost modesty expected of every Jewish girl. Yet, on my wedding night I will be asked to compromise my modesty. How can I give up my purity?" The rabbi replied, "It is for this night you have preserved your innocence."*

This dilemma is even more acute if we consider the laws of marriage as it is presented in the Torah. According to the plain-sense meaning of the text—"When a man takes a wife and is intimate with her"—once a man decides to marry a woman, he is to betroth her first (*kiddushin*) with an act of intimacy, and only later bring her into his home to complete the process and make her his full-fledged wife (*nisuin*). In other words, a Jewish girl, who has been chaste her whole life, is expected to compromise her modesty and relinquish her chastity at the first stage of marriage, while still remaining a member of her father's household, well before she ever moves out to live with her husband. How is a Jewish girl to handle this situation?

- On the one hand, she wants to get married.
- On the other hand, according to the plain-sense meaning of the text, the only way to achieve this is through a radical act that

conflicts with the way she has comported herself throughout her whole life.

Sensitive to this agonizing dilemma, our sages see in the text a way for a girl to negotiate the stages of marriage without drastically compromising her modesty and innocence. At the climax of their negotiations, Avraham says to Ephron, "I am giving the money for the field; take [it] from me, and I will bury my dead there." Since the expression "take [it]" used by Avraham during his negotiations with Ephron refers to money, the same expression, "takes," found in the context of betrothal, say our sages, connotes a transference of money as well. By interpreting the text to allow money to create *kiddushin*, our sages provide a more modest option for a bride. To be sure, come the wedding night (*nisuin*), she will have to give up her chastity. Still, she will do so as an already married woman, who has arrived at this intense moment in gradual phases.

The very money that enables Ephron to deftly negotiate his way through his dilemma, and to save face in front of his people, is transported into the institution of marriage to help a Jewish bride navigate her way through the stages of marriage while preserving her honor and self-respect.

Ki Savo

Avraham's Covenant

WHEN A JEWISH landowner brings his *bikkurim*, seasonal first fruits, to the Beis Hamikdash and places them in gratitude before the altar, he recites a brief synopsis of Jewish history, highlighting our bitter enslavement in Egypt, followed by our redemption by Hashem's mighty hand, and culminating in how He brought us to and gave us the Land of Israel. This sweeping account begins, though, with the tribulations, not of the entire nation, but of one of our forefathers and a certain Aramean:

- According to *Rashi*'s rendition of the text, the farmer recalls how "Lavan, the Aramean, tried to destroy my forefather, Yaakov."[1]
- *Rashi*'s grandson, the *Rashbam*, however, interprets the introduction differently. According to him, the Aramean is our forefather: "Avraham, our forefather, was a wandering Aramean,

---

1   *Devarim* 26:5.

having left his homeland, his birthplace, and his father's home at the behest of Hashem."[2]

Far from only being a dispute over a technical issue of translation, these variant readings of the Jewish narrative reflect fundamentally divergent understandings of the role of Avraham Avinu in world history.

There are two basic ways to cast the covenant between Avraham and Hashem:

- The first approach sees Avraham's covenant as merely an antecedent to the covenant between B'nei Yisrael and Hashem, which was entered into at Har Sinai. From this viewpoint, Avraham's covenant has no independent significance outside the framework of the Tribes of Israel, his descendants that emerged from his grandson, Yaakov Avinu. The covenant, which created a relationship between Avraham and Hashem, evolved into its final form, with its final terms, when B'nei Yisrael and Hashem contracted with each other at the giving of the Torah, the latter covenant superseding the former.

- Alternatively, Avraham's covenant with Hashem has its own integrity. It is a covenant that is independent of the Jewish People, not supplanted by B'nei Yisrael's covenant, and whose relevance extends even after the Revelation at Har Sinai.

This latter perspective finds expression in the teaching of our sages found in *Pirkei Avos*, which lists the five acquisitions Hashem has in this world: Torah, Heaven and Earth, Avraham, Am Yisrael, and the Beis Hamikdash.[3] If Avraham's role in history and covenant are only precursors to Am Yisrael and its mission, it makes no sense to count them as separate fundamental entities "owned" by Hashem. Indeed, the same list found elsewhere, in a midrash, only counts four acquisitions of Hashem, leaving out Avraham.[4] Presumably, this version reflects the dissenting view that Avraham only began a process that reached

---

2   Ibid.

3   *Avos* 6:10.

4   *Mechilta D'Rabi Yishmael, Beshalach* 9.

its climax when his chosen descendants covenanted with Hashem at Har Sinai.

Evidence that Avraham's covenant has independent significance and is more than a forerunner for B'nei Yisrael's covenant can be found in normative law, as well:

- The *bikkurim* declaration recited by a convert
- Eisav's inheritance in the land promised to Avraham
- The obligation of *bris milah* incumbent upon Avraham's children from his second wife, Keturah

The Mishnah in *Bikkurim* states explicitly that while a convert who purchased land in Israel is obligated to bring his first fruits to the Beis Hamikdash, he cannot recite the accompanying declaration, which summarizes Jewish history, "for he cannot honestly say that these fruits come from 'the land that Hashem swore to our forefathers to give to us.'"[5] Yet, the *Yerushalmi* records a dissenting opinion:

> *Rabbi Yehudah taught, a convert brings and recites. What is the justification? "For I have made you (Avraham) the father of a multitude of nations"—until now you were merely a father of Aram; henceforth, you are a father to all nations (to anyone who converts).*[6]

Although converts have no portion in the Land of Israel as members of Am Yisrael, neither in practice nor in theory,[7] they do have a fundamental, virtual share in the Land of Israel as the legal heirs of Avraham.[8] Even before B'nei Yisrael emerged on the scene and the promise made to Avraham, Yitzchak, and Yaakov regarding the land that flows with milk and honey was extended to them, Avraham was promised first that any and all of his legally recognized children would inherit the land.[9] The actual gifting of the land to one specific descendent, Am Yisrael, does

---

5   *Devarim* 26:3; Mishnah *Bikkurim* 1:4.
6   YT *Bikkurim* 1:4.
7   *Sifri Bamidbar Piska* 132.
8   *Ramban*, BT *Bava Basra* 81a.
9   *Rambam, Mishneh Torah,* Laws of First Fruits 4:3.

not render null the original promise that all of Avraham's legal heirs, which include future converts, have a stake in the land too.

The implication is startling: the land that is commonly referred to as "the Land of Israel" overlaps with "the Land of Avraham." Moreover, to qualify for the *bikkurim* recitation, one need neither be a descendent of Israel nor have an actual portion in the Land of Israel. It is equally sufficient to be the descendent of Avraham and have a claim to the Land of Avraham as one of his children, for such a person, too, can genuinely declare that "these fruits come from the land that Hashem swore to our forefathers to give to us." For this reason, the synopsis of Jewish history recited by the farmer begins, according to the *Rashbam*, not with the hardships of Yaakov, the father of B'nei Yisrael, but with the trials of Avraham, the father of all nations. This conceptualization of the mitzvah of *bikkurim* is only coherent if one assumes that Avraham's covenant has significance independent of B'nei Yisrael and the covenant made at Har Sinai.

Aside from converts, there are other legally recognized heirs of Avraham who have a claim to the land promised to him. When B'nei Yisrael were set to make their final journey toward the Promised Land via the land of Seir, Hashem warns them not to provoke "your brothers, the children of Eisav" in an attempt to capture their land, "for as an inheritance to Eisav have I given Mount Seir."[10] Similarly, B'nei Yisrael are warned not to antagonize the children of Lot when they pass by their borders en route to the Land of Canaan, "for I have given them the Land of Ar as an inheritance."[11] From whom was Eisav's and Lot's land bequeathed? *Rashi* answers:

> From Avraham. "I gave him the land of ten nations"[12]—seven
> are for you; and the other three, the Kenite, the Kenizzite, and
> the Kadmonite, which are the lands of Ammon, Moab, and
> Seir, one of them, Seir, is for Eisav, and the other two are for
> the children of Lot as a reward for having gone with Avraham

---

10   *Devarim* 2:4–5.
11   Ibid. 2:9.
12   *Bereishis* 15:19–21.

to Egypt and having kept silent with regard to what Avraham would say about his wife, "She is my sister."[13] *Therefore G-d made Lot as Avraham's son.*

The land promised to Avraham was inhabited by various indigenous peoples and extended well past the borders of the Land of Canaan. Although B'nei Yisrael are the chosen descendants of Avraham, and Yishmael is explicitly *excluded* from being considered Avraham's legal heir when Hashem justifies his expulsion from Avraham's house—"for in Yitzchak will offspring [be] considered yours,"[14] the rest of Avraham's descendants retain vestiges of their legal connection to him. As a result, the main section of the land promised to Avraham was granted to B'nei Yisrael, while other, marginal parts were given to Eisav and Lot.[15]

The *Ramban*, who ascribes to *Rashi's* view, notes that this shared relationship that B'nei Yisrael and the children of Eisav and Lot have with Avraham is underscored by the fact that when the latter conquered their respective portions, they did so in a miraculous fashion just like B'nei Yisrael did when they eventually conquered their share of the land promised to Avraham.[16] Moreover, the *Ramban* asserts that these warnings preventing us from attacking Eisav and Lot to incorporate their lands are immutable, binding for all time. Since Avraham's covenant was not merely a precursor to B'nei Yisrael's covenant, and these lands are part of the "Land of Avraham" promised to him, we have no right to seize them from his other legally recognized heirs to whom they were bequeathed.[17]

---

13   Ibid. 12:19.

14   Ibid. 21:12.

15   See *Netziv*, who observes that only the citizens of Edom, who were given Seir—and not other descendants of Eisav, like Amalek or Kenaz—are considered our brothers and carry Avraham's legacy. See also BT *Sanhedrin* 59b, where Eisav is excluded from being considered a legal heir of Avraham because of *Bereishis* 21:12. Yet, since this exclusion is not explicit, as it is regarding Yishmael, and only alluded to, it reflects a qualification that some descendants of Eisav are considered legal heirs, albeit in a diminished way.

16   *Ramban, Devarim* 2:10.

17   Still, as explained by the *Ramban* in his commentary to the *Rambam's Sefer Hamitzvos*, in the coming days of the Mashiach, these lands will be conquered by us and absorbed into the Land of Israel, but only because Eisav and Lot will have already been displaced by other invading nations.

Avraham's independent status outside the context of Am Yisrael impacts matters that are not related to the land promised him, as well. According to our sages, the sons of Keturah, Avraham's second wife, whom he married after the death of Sarah Imenu, were all circumcised. When Hashem covenants with Avraham regarding *milah*, He warns that any of his male offspring who is not circumcised will be spiritually excised (*kares*), "for he has invalidated My covenant." This latter phrase includes Avraham's future sons given to him by Keturah in the covenant of *milah*.[18] Some commentaries see no novelty in this fact; after all, Avraham was obligated to circumcise all members of his household, including even slaves. Yet, other commentators interpret the teaching to mean that, for all time, Avraham's male descendants from Keturah must be circumcised. As legally recognized children of Avraham, they are perpetually obligated by the covenant made between their forefather and Hashem.[19] Clearly, this latter view, which imposes *bris milah* on Avraham's descendants other than B'nei Yisrael, only makes sense if Avraham's covenant has its own integrity and has significance outside the framework of Am Yisrael.

Until this point, we have demonstrated that Avraham's covenant includes and binds, in some shape or form, his other legally recognized descendants. What still remains to be determined is if his select descendants, B'nei Yisrael, are still bound by his original covenant. In other words: Perhaps, as far as B'nei Yisrael are concerned, their covenant at Har Sinai refined and *replaced* Avraham's covenant. Alternatively, what was contracted at Har Sinai was *in addition* to Avraham's covenant, which is independently and forever binding on any and all his descendants.

Indeed, there is evidence in the laws of *bris milah* that points to the latter view:

- A *bris milah* that should take place on the eighth day, yet does not override the Shabbos
- That the mitzvah of *bris milah* demands two blessings

---

18   BT *Sanhedrin* 59b.
19   *Rambam*, Mishneh Torah, Laws of Kings 10:7–8; *Ran*, BT *Sanhedrin* ibid.

The Gemara assumes that any circumcision that ideally should take place on the eighth day from the child's birth can and should be performed on the Shabbos when they coincide, despite the inevitable Shabbos violation. On the flipside, if a particular case of *bris milah* is not included in the Torah's permission to override the Shabbos, such as a caesarean birth, then there is no requirement to be circumcised on the eighth day specifically, even if it falls on a weekday.[20] However, the *Rambam* codifies the law to the contrary, that there are scenarios, such as a caesarean birth, where the child should be circumcised on the eighth day specifically, but not if it coincides with Shabbos![21]

Rabbi Chaim Soloveitchik explains that the principle that links the eighth day requirement and the permit to override Shabbos only governs the mitzvah of *milah* that was commanded to B'nei Yisrael on Har Sinai: "On the eighth day, the flesh of his foreskin shall be circumcised."[22] Our sages derive from the definite article, "*the* eighth day," that Shabbos is superseded by an eighth-day *milah*.[23] However, the *bris milah* that is a sign of Avraham's covenant is not subject to this standard. The *bris milah* given to Avraham, which predates and is independent of the covenant and mitzvah of *milah* of Har Sinai, is not conceptually tethered to the issue of Shabbos at all. Since Hashem commanded Avraham to circumcise members of his household and all future generations "at the age of eight days,"[24] that is still expected of his descendants. Consequently, a caesarean-born baby is circumcised on the eighth day specifically. This is so even if it would not be performed on the eighth day should it and Shabbos coincide.[25]

That B'nei Yisrael are obligated to perform *bris milah* for two separate reasons and are bound by two covenants—the covenant of Avraham

---

20   BT *Shabbos* 135a–b.
21   *Mishneh Torah*, Laws of Milah 1:10.
22   *Vayikra* 12:3.
23   BT *Shabbos* 132a.
24   *Bereishis* 17:12.
25   Rabbi Chaim Soloveitchik, in his novelle to *Rambam, Mishneh Torah*, Laws of Milah ibid. How this interpretation of the *Rambam* is compatible with his remarks in the *Laws of Aveilus* 1:1 and in his commentary to the Mishnah in *Chullin* 7:6 is beyond the scope of this work.

and the covenant of Har Sinai—is also reflected in the two blessings we recite when performing the ritual:

1. "That He sanctified us with His mitzvos and commanded us regarding *milah*"
2. "That He sanctified us with His mitzvos and commanded us to enter him into the covenant of Avraham Avinu"

No other mitzvah has two accompanying blessings.[26] *Bris milah* is an exception because it is a fulfillment of two independent identities and obligations:

1. B'nei Yisrael, as descendants of Avraham, Yitzchak and Yaakov, bound by the covenant at Har Sinai
2. B'nei Yisrael, as descendants of Avraham, bound by his original covenant

When Avraham's name was changed from Avram to Avraham to signal that he had been made "the father of a multitude of nations," he was given a Divine mission to spread monotheism throughout the world. Hashem covenanted with Avraham for him to be the catalyst to bring about the objective of creation: that all peoples would recognize the honor of Hashem and that He would reign as King over all the nations of the earth.[27]

To what extent the covenant of Har Sinai demands of B'nei Yisrael to attract converts to a life of Torah and mitzvos or even to simply spread the idea of monotheism is debatable. What should be clear by now, however, is that Avraham's covenant has independent significance and is operative even after Har Sinai. As a result, B'nei Yisrael, descendants of Avraham, are certainly expected to carry his legacy and inspire the nations of the world to recognize and revere the one true G-d, Hashem.

---

26   The blessings of *Shehechiyanu* and *She'asah Nissim* are recited for entirely different reasons and are not relevant to this discussion.

27   *Netziv, Bereishis* 17:4; see also his comments to *Vayikra* 27:44–45 and *Devarim* 27:5.

Nitzavim

Does the Earth Belong to the Living?

ALTHOUGH HE IS known as the father of the Declaration of Independence, Thomas Jefferson was conspicuously absent from the historic Constitutional Convention of 1787, having been assigned to France as an ambassador on behalf of the newly emancipated colonies for much of the 1780s. The epithet, the father of the Constitution, would instead be earned by his fellow Virginian and protégé, James Madison. That decade was a time of great political change, both in the States and in France, when political philosophical ideas were on the mind of anyone who was someone. Jefferson was no different, and wanting to remain relevant while his country was shaping its future, he kept an ongoing correspondence with Madison.

In one such letter, Jefferson ponders a fundamental question he assumes "never to have been started either on this or our side of the water." Jefferson asked "whether one generation of men has a right to bind another" through legislation, and took it for granted that "the earth always belongs to the living generation" because "one generation is to another as one independent nation to another." In his view, a nation consists of an arbitrary collection of individuals who negotiate amongst themselves their rights and obligations. These laws, therefore, are only legally binding on these individuals who currently comprise the nation, for they alone decided them. Once, however, a new collection of individuals arises to constitute the nation, the previous set of laws automatically expire and must be renewed, implicitly or through new negotiations. Just like one nation cannot compel another independent nation to obey its constitution, a society cannot create a perpetual body of law to be implemented from one generation to the next. If it were to do so, argued Jefferson, the current generation would be governed not by right, but by force.[1]

Yet, in actuality, Jefferson was not the first to wonder about the political reach of any given generation. This line of thought was already explored by his contemporary, Thomas Paine. In his book, *The Great Debate: Edmund Burke, Thomas Paine, and the Birth of Right and Left*, political analyst Yuval Levin outlines the broad philosophical differences between Thomas Paine and Edmund Burke. While Paine was a revolutionary, who ardently believed that the only way to correct an unjust society is to overturn it and start from scratch, Burke was a gradual reformer, who appreciated the complexities of society and anticipated unintended consequences as a result of unraveling the fabric of a culture abruptly. Where Paine revered reason and saw no other way but to apply its conclusions in a calculated and impartial way, Burke valued a society's sentiments toward institutions, symbols, and tradition, something detached reason does not consider.

These two intellectual giants also debated the "issue of generations":

- Paine denied the significance of generations, the idea that a current generation shares an identity with those that come before it

---

1   Sept. 6, 1789. Jefferson defined a "generation" as nineteen years.

and is obligated to perpetuate that legacy and pass it on to those that will come after it. Instead, Paine embraced, exclusively, the value and the rights and the freedom of the individual. Like Jefferson, Paine conceived a society as a collection of individuals. He insisted that "we are all, in essence, Adams and Eves—best understood as directly created by our Maker, not as descendants from prior generations." [2] Consequently, no generation had the power to impose legislation on the next.

- Burke, on the other hand, recognized the continuity of generations, the idea that a person is born into a collective, with its unique character and institutions. Society, he said, is an "ongoing partnership between past, present, and future generations."[3]

In truth, however, neither Jefferson nor his contemporaries were the first to consider how to conceptualize a nation—as a group of interdependent individuals or as a collective with its own integrity that transcends the individuals that constitute it. As a comprehensive blueprint of society, the Torah has its own political philosophy, which is expressed in its laws and narratives, sometimes explicitly, at other times implicitly.

At the very end of Moshe Rabbeinu's life, he gathers the entire nation at the border of the Land of Israel to renew their covenant with Hashem: He will make us His people and He will be our G-d, as promised to our forefathers. Moshe then makes it clear that this pact is perpetual.

I make this covenant, with its sanctions, not with you alone, but both with those who are standing here with us this day before Hashem our God and with those who are not with us here this day.[4]

---

2   Thomas Paine, *Rights of Man: Being an Answer to Mr. Burke's Attack on the French Revolution* (1791). Paine, in an earlier treatment of the issue, defined a "generation" as thirty years, *Dissertations on Government: The Affairs of the Bank; and Paper Money* (1786).

3   Cited in Yuval Levin, *The Great Debate: Edmund Burke, Thomas Paine, and the Birth of Right and Left* (Basic Books, 2013).

4   *Devarim* 29:13–4.

Although it is expressed elegantly, the legal justification for what Moshe asserts—that future generations will be legally bound by the commitment of this generation—is elusive. Does a given generation indeed have political power over future generations? The midrash, undoubtedly bothered by this legal conundrum, finesses the apparent legal difficulty by imagining that all the souls of future generations were present and participated in the covenant. Though their bodies were not "standing here today," their souls were in attendance.[5]

If we were to interpret the midrash literally—that the souls of all the Jews throughout history were actually there—then the midrash would be anticipating and siding with the viewpoint of Jefferson and Paine. Legally, no group of individuals, even if they constitute a nation, can enforce their will on other individuals not yet extant. The only reason why in this instance this was seemingly acceptable was because no one was truly absent. Everyone who would be affected by this commitment participated and approved.

The *Abarbanel*, however, interprets the midrash figuratively. Yet, he too belongs to the same school of political thought as Jefferson and Paine. Three centuries before Jefferson, the Abarbanel also pondered the "issue of generations" and concluded that no group of individuals can rightfully compel another group of individuals to fulfill the former's past commitments, even if they belong to the same nation in succession. The *Abarbanel*, therefore, was forced to identify another legal framework to justify the perpetual nature of the covenant. He found it in servanthood. According to the *Abarbanel*, the binding mechanism of the covenant was not the oath but ownership. Having redeemed us from Egypt, Hashem acquired us and became our new Master. As the verse says, "For it is to Me that the Israelites are servants: they are My servants, whom I freed from the land of Egypt."[6] Since a master owns not only his slave but any offspring produced from that slave, Hashem, likewise, has title not only of every Jew who was present at the formalization of the covenant but of any and every Jew born from

---

5   *Tanchuma, Devarim* 8.
6   *Vayikra* 25:55.

then onwards. This is the meaning of the midrash when it describes that all the souls of future generations were present at the covenant: the obligation of future generations to Hashem had been latent in their ancestors' status as servants.

A century later, the *Maharal* took the significance of the midrash one step further. Like the Abarbanel, he interprets the midrash figuratively. Yet, unlike the Abarbanel who perceives the Jewish nation as a collection of interdependent individuals, the *Maharal* conceptualizes the nation as a single organic entity with a unique character and continuity of identity that is perpetuated from generation to generation. This is the deeper meaning behind the image that all the souls of future generations were present at the time of the covenant. When B'nei Yisrael entered into the covenant with Hashem, it wasn't affected by a multitude of discrete individuals on one side and Hashem on the other. Rather, the pact was affected on another plane of existence, between only two parties: the nation of Israel, and Hashem. As a result, any individual born into the nation, by dint of his or her membership in the nation, is bound to the covenant. By conceptualizing a nation as a collective, an independent entity with an integrity greater than the sum of its parts, the *Maharal* discovers the legal justification for one generation to create a perpetual law and allegiance that binds all future generations who are identified with the nation.[7]

In the final analysis, we can suggest that both the *Abarbanel* (Jefferson and Paine) and the *Maharal* (Burke) are right. The following midrash notices a subtle difference between the way the Torah presents the family of Eisav and the family of Yaakov. The former is described in the plural, the latter in the singular:

> *With regard to Eisav we find six souls are written in association with him and language suggesting many souls is written in association with him, as is written, "Eisav took his wives,*

---

7   *Maharal, Netzach Yisrael* 11.

his sons, his daughters, and nafshos (all the souls) of his household."[8]

And, by contrast, we find that in association with Yaakov, seventy souls are recorded and, yet, language suggesting only one soul is written in association with him, as is written, "And all the persons who emerged from Yaakov's loins were seventy nafesh (one soul)."[9]

When we consider how to define a gentile nation, the *Abarbanel's* conceptualization is correct: each nation is merely a collection of individuals, each of its members an independent "Adam or Eve," with no antecedent and no obligation to the past. However, as the *Maharal* asserts, when we look to the Jewish nation, we encounter something qualitatively different: like a human being whose identity and personality transcend the cells that animate him, the nation of Israel is an organism with its own soul and character that is kept alive by the minds and bodies of its members, one generation to the next.

---

8   *Bereishis* 36:6.
9   *Shemos* 1:5; *Vayikra Rabbah* 4:6.

Vayelech

Hakhel: The State of the Union Address

IN THE EIGHTEENTH century, political philosophers debated the nature of sovereignty, i.e., whether it can be shared or not. The union between Britain and Scotland, as well as the ongoing power struggle between the British Crown and Parliament, necessitated a discussion about the possibility of multiple entities ruling over one body politic, each having its own political sphere that it controls exclusively. Foreshadowing the federal system that would find expression in the constitution of the United States of America—which assigns different powers to the national and state governments that, together, were sovereigns over the country's citizens—many political thinkers argued that, indeed, sovereignty can be shared. Others, however, asserted that, by definition, supreme authority cannot be shared. Only one source can be invested with absolute power. These political theorists were not the first to explore this issue because it was debated thousands of years earlier between none other than…Moshe Rabbeinu and Hashem Himself!

On the day of his death, Moshe charges Yehoshua in front of all the people to "be strong and courageous, for you shall come with this people to the land Hashem swore to their forefathers to give them."[1] However, when Hashem commands Yehoshua directly, there is a subtle difference. Instead of implying, as Moshe does, that Yehoshua will merely accompany the people to the land, Hashem suggests that Yehoshua will play a more active role and lead them: "Be strong and courageous, for you shall bring B'nei Yisrael to the land that I have sworn to them."[2] Our sages explain the discrepancy as follows:

> *Moshe said to Yehoshua, "The elders of the generation shall be with you. Everything should be done in accordance with their opinion and advice." But the Holy One, Blessed is He, said to Yehoshua, "Bring them without their having a choice in the matter. Everything depends on you. If necessary, take a rod and hit them on the crown of the head. There is one leader for a generation, and not two leaders for a generation."*[3]

While Moshe assumes that the king (Yehoshua) and the national Supreme Court (the elders) will share power and lead the nation together, Hashem envisions that the nation will be led by one supreme authority, the king. Unlike Moshe who thinks sovereignty can be shared, with different bodies overseeing and answering to each other, Hashem insists that absolute power, by definition, *cannot* be distributed.

Why, though, does the Torah present these opposing views in such a subtle way, barely noticeable to the reader? Moreover, even if we assume that Hashem's view, after all, is right, it is odd that the Torah never explicitly dismisses Moshe's opinion.

We can suggest that the Torah treats the issue in a nuanced way because the Torah's political philosophy regarding sovereignty is more

---

1   *Devarim* 31:7.
2   Ibid. 31:23.
3   BT *Sanhedrin* 8a, as quoted by *Rashi, Devarim* 31:7.

nuanced than an either-or approach. For this reason, the Torah never rejects Moshe's opinion outright because it, too, is legitimate, as it expresses an aspect of the Torah's political theory. Where, though, does the Torah formulate its nuanced position regarding the distribution of power? We do not have to go too far. The Torah mediates between Moshe's and Hashem's perspectives in the very section that separates (and bridges) Moshe's and Hashem's summoning of Yehoshua: the mitzvah of *hakhel*.

After Moshe summons and speaks to Yehoshua, he entrusts his *Sefer Torah* to the Kohanim and Elders of Israel and then turns his attention to the mitzvah of *hakhel*:

> *Moshe commanded them, saying, "At the end of seven years, at the time of the shemittah year, during the Sukkos festival, when all Israel comes to appear before Hashem, your G-d, in the place that He will choose, you shall read this Torah before all Israel, in their ears. Gather together the people—the men, and the women, and the small children, and the stranger who is in your cities—so that they will hear and so that they will learn, and they shall fear Hashem, your G-d, and be careful to perform all the words of this Torah. And their children who do not know—they shall learn to fear Hashem, your G-d, all the days that you live on the land to which you are crossing the Jordan, to take possession of it."*[4]

Although the command *to gather* the entire nation and *to read* from the Torah once every seven years is expressed in the singular, there is a disagreement about how to render the verses:

- *Targum Onkelos* translates them as they appear, in the singular, leading the *Chizkuni* to interpret that Moshe is addressing Yehoshua directly. Consequently, the *Chizkuni* derives from the text itself the obligation that the king is supposed to read from

---

4   *Devarim* 31:10–13.

the Torah at the *hakhel* ceremony.[5] Similarly, *Rashi* interprets the plain-sense meaning of "you shall read this Torah" as enjoining, specifically, the king to read.[6]

- *Targum Yonasan*, however, translates the verbs "to read" and "to gather" in the plural. After all, Moshe had just finished handing over his *Sefer Torah* to the Kohanim and elders, and his subsequent command concerning *hakhel* was addressed "to them."[7] Only for stylistic reasons does the Torah address all the leaders of the nation in the singular. According to this rendition, the mitzvah of *hakhel*, along with its concomitant obligation to read from the Torah, is incumbent upon all the leaders of the nation, including but not limited to the king.[8] This interpretation of the mitzvah is supported by the fact that the passage of *hakhel* is not included in the passage of the king recorded elsewhere in *Sefer Devarim*.

According to *Rashi* and the *Chizkuni*, we can only wonder why the mitzvah of *hakhel* is presented where it is, and not there with the rest of the regulations and obligations of the king.

Still, even according to *Targum Yonasan*, the Oral Torah does teach that it is truly the king's responsibility to read for the assembled at *hakhel* from the *Sefer Torah*.[9] Where in the Written Torah is this law alluded to? Fittingly, the source is derived from the portion of the Torah that outlines the institution of the king. There, the Torah commands: "When [the king] is seated on his royal throne, he shall have a copy of this teaching written for him on a scroll...let it remain with him and let him read in it all his life."[10] Our sages derive two laws that relate to *hakhel* from this verse:

---

5   *Chizkuni, Devarim* ibid. See BT *Sotah* 41a.
6   *Rashi, Devarim* ibid.
7   Hashem's summoning of Yehoshua is also followed by Moshe entrusting his Torah scroll to his tribe, Levi, for safekeeping, to be placed next to the Ark of the Covenant of Hashem.
8   Rabbi Yerucham F. Perlow develops this approach in his commentary to Rabbi Saadia Gaon's list of 613 mitzvos, *personal positive mitzvah* no. 15 and *communal mitzvah* no. 10.
9   *Sotah* 7:8.
10   *Devarim* 17:18.

- The king should write a *sefer* for himself so that he can read from it at all the *hakhel* ceremonies throughout his life and reign.[11]
- The *sefer* he is obligated to write for himself and read from is only *Sefer Devarim*, not an entire *Sefer Torah*.[12]

What emerges according to *Targum Yonasan* is that the Torah has two separate treatments of *hakhel*, each one suggesting a completely different version than the other:

- **The passage of *hakhel* (*Devarim* 31):** *Hakhel* is organized by the nation's various leaders—the king, supreme court judges, tribal princes, and the Kohanim. The reading from the Torah is performed by the recognized, most outstanding leading figure of the generation as an agent of the entire leadership. When there is a king, he naturally fits that description, but he reads only as a first among equals. Although the reading is of select passages,[13] it is done using a complete *Sefer Torah*. The actual scroll that is used is the original one Moshe Rabbeinu wrote and entrusted to the Kohanim for safekeeping, stored on the Temple Mount.[14]
- **The passage of the king (*Devarim* 17):** The king is especially responsible to organize the ceremony and read from the Torah for the assembled. He reads from select passages, but does so from his own private scroll, which is composed of *Sefer Devarim* alone.

How are we to reconcile these discrepancies? Moreover, why is the presentation of *hakhel* in the passage of *hakhel* explicit, part of the Written Torah, while the one in the passage of the king only implied and taught through the Oral Torah?

Because of these difficulties, many early commentators are compelled to count these two passages as two distinct mitzvos in the list of the 613 Mitzvos:

---

11   Cited in Rabbi Perlow, ibid.
12   Ibid.
13   *Sotah* ibid.
14   As implied by the text. See also *Rashi*, BT *Bava Basra* 14b, *d"h Sefer Azarah*.

- The Written Torah's explicit description of the ceremony details the *nation*'s mitzvah of *hakhel*, which is the default, unadulterated version of the event.
- The Oral Torah's implicit, derived description of the ceremony, on the other hand, details the king's *personal* mitzvah of *hakhel*, which gives him the prerogative to alter the *hakhel* ceremony according to his discretion.

The objective of the nation's mitzvah of *hakhel* is to inspire religious growth, engender national pride, and strengthen unity.[15] Still, as important as these agendas are, they are general, ill-defined goals. Sometimes a nation needs more specific direction and precisely defined goals.

Therefore, every seven years, the king is obligated to assess the health of his people and determine whether the standard *hakhel* ceremony is enough to maintain and further his nation's ambitions. If it is, then the king assumes a more passive part in the process, emphasizing not his political power, but his role as a national symbol. He, along with the rest of the nation's leadership, gather the people. Although the king does the reading, it is done using a national treasure, the ancient scroll written by Moshe himself, and he does so as an agent of the people and its leadership, leveraging his crown as an inspirational and unifying force. The king, under these circumstances, might even forego his exclusive, royal privilege to sit in the Temple Courtyard. Instead, as a reflection of his political partnership with the rest of the nation's leadership, he could stand while reading from the Torah, a gesture found to be praiseworthy in the estimation of our sages.[16] This demonstration and organization of political power is the vision Moshe Rabbeinu shares with Yehoshua: sovereignty can be shared and distributed.

However, if, after assessing the state of his nation, the king is unnerved by what he sees, having identified certain flaws and cracks, he is obligated not to remain idle but to react by using the *hakhel* ceremony as his forum to articulate a specific agenda, announce new public

---

15   *Sefer Hachinuch* 612; *Kli Yakar, Devarim* ibid; Rabbi Shimshon Raphael Hirsch, *Devarim* ibid.
16   BT *Sotah* 41a.

policies, and demand compliance. Under these circumstances, the king reads from his own private scroll, composed strictly of *Sefer Devarim*. Like Moshe Rabbeinu, who composed *Sefer Devarim* to outline for B'nei Yisrael what he thought they needed in order to successfully conquer, settle, and cultivate the Land of Israel, the king reads select portions from his personal scroll of *Sefer Devarim*[17] to frame his address about the state of his nation. To further his agenda, the king, if he deems it necessary, might invoke his prerogative and specifically sit while reading from his scroll to project formidability and instill fear in those assembled. In this role, the king is not representing the nation's body of leadership, but acting as an absolute monarch, imposing his will on all the country's citizens—leaders and commoners alike. The king has this right and responsibility because, fundamentally, as Hashem informed Yehoshua, there is one leader for a generation, and not two leaders for a generation.

Soon after the nation of Israel is split into two, the Northern (Israel) and Southern (Yehudah) Kingdoms, Yeravam, the king of Israel, erects two shrines at the northern and southern tips of his kingdom. His motive is to establish a legitimate alternative to the Beis Hamikdash, located in Yerushalayim, the capital of the Kingdom of Yehudah. Yeravam goes to great lengths to prevent his people from making the pilgrimage to Yerushalayim during the Festival of Sukkos in the first year of his reign. Not only does he position guards blocking the roads to Yerushalayim, giving travelers no choice but to pay homage at either of the two new shrines,[18] but he also intercalates an additional month into his kingdom's calendar to deceive his people, causing them to miscalculate when the Festival of Sukkos would be celebrated in the Southern Kingdom.[19]

Our sages explain that Yeravam went through such trouble because he feared the political fallout of a pilgrimage to Yerushalayim. The year was a *hakhel* year. Yeravam knew that his rival, Rechavam, the

---

17   *Emes L'Yaakov, Devarim* ibid.

18   BT *Taanis* 30b.

19   *Melachim I* 12:33.

king of Yehudah, would exploit the opportunity and take advantage of the king's prerogative to use *hakhel* as a platform to launch a political agenda—in this case, to reunite the people under Rechavam's exclusive rule. Likewise, Yeravam concluded that Rechavam would undoubtedly choose to sit in the Temple Courtyard during his reading from the Torah scroll, while the rest of the people, including Yeravam, would be forced to stand in deference to the Beis Hamikdash, Hashem, and His true representative, King Rechavam.[20] This scene would not only humiliate Yeravam, it would ensure the success of Rechavam's reunification plan, predicated on the political theory that sovereignty truly cannot be shared.

Yet, Rechavam could have taken an alternative course. He might have discharged his royal duties differently. As we have seen, *hakhel* comes in different forms. Rechavam, humbled by the people's rebellion, chastened by a house divided, and acutely aware that the schism was ordained by Hashem,[21] may have organized a *hakhel* that did not emphasize the king's absolute authority, but, rather, national unity under political partnership. Alas, we never got the chance to find out.

---

20   BT *Sanhedrin* 102a.

21   *Melachim I* 12:24.

Ha'azinu

Birkas HaTorah: Praise or Permission?

IN THE JEWISH tradition, there are three kinds of blessings we recite:

1. Before we derive pleasure from Hashem's world (*birkas ha'nehenin*)
2. Before we perform a commandment (*birkas ha'mitzvah*)
3. In order to express praise and thanksgiving to Hashem (*birkas shevach v'hoda'ah*)[1]

Although the justification for the first and last categories is readily understandable, the requirement to recite a blessing before we perform a mitzvah is more elusive. Many classic commentators understand the rationale behind this blessing in light of the third category of blessings: we recite a blessing before we perform rituals to praise and thank

---

1   *Rambam, Mishneh Torah*, Laws of Blessings 1:4.

Hashem for sanctifying us and enriching our lives with His mitzvos. By doing so, we put ourselves in the right frame of mind, enabling us to perform Hashem's mitzvos with solemnity and not cavalierly.

The *Rambam*, however, conceptualizes the blessing recited before mitzvos in terms of the first category: "Anyone who derives pleasure without first making a blessing is considered as if he stole from Hashem...and just like we make a blessing before enjoying this world, so too, we make a blessing on each and every mitzvah we plan to fulfill and only afterwards do we perform it."[2] In what way are these two categories comparable? Rabbi Yosef Soloveitchik explains that there is a theological problem inherent in both of these activities, respectively. On the one hand, eating and enjoyment are necessary for our physical and mental wellbeing. On the other hand, what we intend to make use of to derive these pleasures is not ours but owned by Hashem. Ultimately, the very awareness of this tension and the verbal acknowledgement that everything belongs to Hashem, as expressed in the blessing, gives us the license to partake of His world.

Similarly, when it comes to observing Hashem's commandments, we face a conundrum. On the one hand, we have a spiritual need to bond with Hashem by fulfilling his mitzvos. On the other hand, how can finite, fallible, mortal man consider to associate and approach, let alone connect, to the infinite, inscrutable, immortal G-d? To attempt, even, to bridge this immeasurable gap is nothing short of hubris. Yet, by being conscious of this conflict and articulating that our ambitions are sanctioned by G-d Himself, we are granted the permit to relate to Him.

Interestingly, the only *birkas ha'mitzvah* that the Torah mandates is the one recited before we study Torah, known as *birkas haTorah*. The source for this requirement is found in the preamble of Moshe's song, *Ha'azinu*: "When I call out the Name of Hashem, ascribe greatness to our G-d."[3] According to the *Ramban*, the impetus of this blessing is to praise and give thanks to Hashem for singling us out and giving us the Torah. In other words, conceptually, the only *birkas ha'mitzvah*

---

2   *Mishneh Torah* ibid. 1:3.

3   *Devarim* 32:3; BT *Berachos* 21a.

that the Torah enjoins us to recite is fundamentally a *birkas shevach v'hoda'ah*.[4] Some commentators maintain that the blessing we recite before learning Torah is essentially a *birkas ha'nehenin*. The intellectual stimulation experienced when exposed to the truth and wisdom of the Torah demands a blessing no less than when we enjoy other pleasures of this world.[5] Still others assume that *birkas haTorah* is a classic *birkas ha'mitzvah* and is recited before we engage in the mitzvah of Talmud Torah to ensure we have the proper mindset when we study it, not to do so as an academic pursuit but as a spiritual endeavor.

In light of the *Rambam*'s formulation analyzed above, which frames a *birkas ha'mitzvah* as a permit to engage with Hashem, we can suggest another reason why the Torah requires a blessing before we learn Torah. The *Ramban*, in his introduction to *Sefer Bereishis*, reveals a deep secret about the text of the Torah:

> We also possess a true tradition that the Torah in its entirety consists of Names of the Holy One, Blessed is He. For the words of the Torah can be divided in a different way into other words...namely, that the writing was a stream of contiguous letters, without division into words, so that it was possible, when it was read, to be read in the manner of Divine Names or to be read in the manner of our reading, which concerns the Torah and the commandments, as we read it today.[6]

Remarkably, every time we open a Torah and read from it, we encounter the Names of Hashem embedded in the text. This is highly significant, for names, in our tradition, are not merely convenient labels that facilitate communication, but are reflections of the essence of the entity to which they refer. Exposure to Hashem's Names, then, is an intimate experience with Hashem Himself. Whatever his motive, how could mortal man ever consider that he has the right to behold and

---

4   *Ramban* in his commentary to *Rambam*'s *Sefer Hamitzvos*.

5   Based on the comments of Rabbi Avraham min haHar's novella to BT *Nedarim* 48a and *Eglei Tal*, Introduction.

6   *Ramban*, introduction to *Bereishis*.

experience even a glimpse of the essence of the Master of the Universe? Such audacity is astounding. The license to do so, however, is granted to those that recite *birkas haTorah* before studying the Torah: "When I call out the Name of Hashem"—the text of the Torah, which is a long string of Hashem's Names, "ascribe greatness to our G-d"—recite a blessing beforehand. By expressing that we only dare engage with Hashem's essence because he sanctified and commanded us to do so, we avoid any act of hubris.[7]

Our sages debate which type of Torah study demands a *birkas haTorah*:

> *Rav Huna said: "For mikra [Biblical text] one must recite a blessing; for midrash [derivations of law teased out of the text] one does not need to recite a blessing." Rabbi Elazar said: "For mikra and midrash one must recite a blessing; for Mishnah [code of law] one need not recite a blessing." Rabbi Yochanan said: "For Mishnah one must recite a blessing as well, but for Talmud [analysis of the Mishnah] one need not recite a blessing." Rava said: "Even for Talmud one must recite a blessing."[8]*

While an analysis of all four opinions is beyond the scope of this work, based on our discussion of *birkas haTorah*, we can explain the debate between the two extreme views as follows. Rav Huna, who severely limits the scope of the obligation, assumes:

- The recitation of a blessing before Torah study is based on the need for a permit to do the unthinkable: to share an intimacy with Hashem;
- Only an engagement with the actual letters and words of the Torah (*mikra*) is considered an encounter with Hashem's essence, because the text of the Torah comprises Hashem's Names.

---

7   This approach is inspired by the thought of Rabbi Chaim Soloveitchik, Rabbi Yosef Soloveitchik's grandfather, regarding *birkas haTorah*, quoted in his son's, Rabbi Yitzchak Zev Soloveitchik's novella to the *Rambam's Mishneh Torah*.

8   BT *Berachos* 11b.

Rava, who subjects any kind of Torah study to the obligation of *birkas haTorah*, concludes as he does because he challenges either of Rav Huna's two assumptions:

- Perhaps, Rava argues with Rav Huna's first assumption, and anticipates the view that the blessing recited before Torah study is a *birkas ha'nehenin*, permitting the pleasure enjoyed when learning Torah, which certainly applies to the more sophisticated and intellectually stimulating study of Talmud.
- Or, maybe, Rava contends that the recitation of a blessing is a way to ensure proper motivation, that when one studies the rigorous Talmud he does so not for purely academic reasons, but for spiritual growth.

Alternatively, we can maintain that Rava agrees with Rav Huna's first assumption, that *birkas haTorah* is indeed a needed license allowing mortal man to connect intimately with Hashem. Yet, Rava challenges the second assumption that only an encounter with the Written Torah, whose letters constitute Hashem's Names, exposes man to Hashem's essence. According to Rava, the entire Torah, the Written and Oral Torah, its repository of laws, principles, and values, all are expressions of the mind and heart of Hashem. Consequently, any form of Torah study is an intimacy with Hashem.

The Torah describes the conjugal relations between Adam and Chavah as an act in which "Adam knew Chavah."[9] Intimacy connotes more than a physical connection; it also means a profound familiarity with the other, a meeting of spirits, and a merging of identity. The *Zohar* states, "Hashem, Torah, and those who are immersed in Torah are one."[10] The act of Talmud Torah provides us with an unexpected privilege: to become one with the Only One.

---

9 *Bereishis* 4:1.
10 Quoted in *Ruach Chaim* 6:3.

V'Zos Haberachah

Epilogue: Enlightened

IT'S BACKWARDS. The sacred parchment that is inserted behind the Kohen Gadol's Breastplate is known as "the *Urim* and the *Tumim*."[1]

> *Why is it called Urim and Tumim? Urim, which is based on the word ohr, light, is so-called because it illuminates and explains its words. Tumim, which is based on the word tam, completed, is because it fulfills its words, which always come true.*[2]

Whenever the leadership of the nation needed guidance, it would turn to the Kohen Gadol and present its question to him while he wore the Breastplate. The answer to their inquiry would be Divinely conveyed through the illumination of specific letters engraved on the twelve precious gems set in the Breastplate. The Kohen Gadol, divinely

---

1   *Shemos* 28:30.
2   BT *Yoma* 73b.

inspired,[3] would then decipher the letters to form a coherent message.[4] Its prediction would always come true.

Throughout the Torah, this sacred parchment is referred to as the "the *Urim* and the *Tumim*" in that precise order.[5] Yet, when Moshe blesses the tribe of Levi, he flips the order: "Of Levi, he said:[6] Your *Tumim* and Your *Urim* befit Your devout one."[7] Why?

The *Maharil Diskin* explains that Moshe reverses the order because Moshe is talking *to Hashem* about the tribe of Levi, and from Hashem's perspective, the entire order of the procedure is indeed reversed:

- Normally, when the question is posed to the Kohen Gadol, first, the appropriate letters are miraculously illuminated—*Urim*. Then, the Kohen Gadol, endowed with Divine Spirit, must arrange the chosen letters properly in order to discern the complete—*Tumim*—message.[8] Consequently, throughout the Torah, when the Torah gives instructions to the Kohanim regarding the sacred parchment or describes the actual procedure, it calls the parchment "the *Urim* and the *Tumim*."

- However, from Hashem's standpoint, the matter is already known in its completeness—*Tumim*. Hashem, though, has to enlighten us by Divinely illuminating—*Urim*—the Breastplate. As a result, here, when Moshe addresses Hashem about the compatibility of the tribe of Levi and its sacred task, he reverses the order: "Your *Tumim* and Your *Urim*."

Hashem has blessed us by giving us the light of the Torah.[9] Like the Kohen Gadol, we are expected not only to bask in the Divine light but to discern its meaning in order to become truly enlightened. Hopefully,

---

3   BT *Yoma* ibid., as understood by the *Maharil Diskin* in his commentary to *Devarim* 33:8.
4   BT *Yoma* ibid., according to the opinion of Rabbi Yochanan, as understood by the *Maharil Diskin*.
5   *Shemos* 28:30, *Vayikra* 8:8, *Ezra* 2:63, and *Nechemiah* 7:65.
6   *Rashi, Devarim* 33:8, interprets that Moshe was not talking *to* Levi, but speaking *of* Levi.
7   *Devarim* ibid.
8   Here, the *Maharil Diskin* slightly deviates from the plain-sense meaning of the Gemara in *Yoma*, quoted above, regarding the significance of the name *Tumim*.
9   *Mishlei* 6:23.

our discussions, which have spanned a wide range of the human experience and Torah thought, have enhanced our appreciation and awe of the Torah, contributed to our understanding of the timeless messages of the Torah, and highlighted how the Torah is truly a blueprint for the ideal human society. *May we soon build it and behold it!*

About the Author

RABBI BARUCH DOV BRAUN is the rabbi of the Young Israel of Avenue J in Brooklyn, New York. He received his *semichah* from Yeshiva University's Rabbi Isaac Elchanan Theological Seminary (RIETS), where he was a member of the Wexner Kollel Elyon. He is also a *dayan* on the Brooklyn branch of the Manhattan Beth Din for Conversions. After receiving his *semichah*, Rabbi Braun earned a master's degree in social work from New York University's Silver School of Social Work, where he studied social policy and clinical psychology, and he currently provides psychotherapy in an outpatient mental health clinic. Rabbi Braun's first book, *A Time to Seek*, elucidates the timeless truths of the Torah in contemporary terms.

Rabbi Braun lives with his wife and children in Brooklyn, New York. He welcomes your comments at rabbi.bbraun@gmail.com.

MOSAICA PRESS
BOOK PUBLISHERS

Elegant, Meaningful & Bold

info@MosaicaPress.com
www.MosaicaPress.com

The Mosaica Press team of
acclaimed editors and designers
is attracting some of the most
compelling thinkers and teachers
in the Jewish community today.
Our books are available around
the world.

HARAV YAACOV HABER
RABBI DORON KORNBLUTH